The WONDERFUL WORLD of

OZ

An Illustrated History of the American Classic

John Fricke

Images from The Willard Carroll/Tom Wilhite Collection

Camden, Maine

For my mother, Dorothy, the first and —
all apologies to Baum — the best.
—Willard Carroll

For my parents, Wally and Dottie Fricke — who encouraged
my every moment spent in Oz and who always did
everything they could to make our real world as equally
magical, blessed, and happy a land of love.
— John Fricke

For my parents, Norman and Alice Wilhite
—Tom Wilhite
∞

Copyright 2013 by Willard Carroll and Tom Wilhite
This Down East Books edition is an expanded, revised, and redesigned republication of the edition entitled *100 Years of Oz* published in 1999 by Stewart, Tabori & Chang.

Photographs: Mark Hill: pgs. 16-17 (top), 20, 38, 46, 50, 51, 53 (top), 55, 56 (top), 58, 64 (bottom right), 65, 70, 71 (top right), 73, 75 (top left), 76, 77 (top), 79 (insert), 92, 94-95 (background), 100, 110-111 (background), 114, 116, 118-119 (bottom), 120, 128 (bottom), 129, 130, 133, 140, 142, 144 (top), 148, 153. Additional photography by Richard Glenn.

ISBN 978-1-60893-257-3

Designed by Lynda Chilton
Production services by Down East Enterprise, Inc.

Down East Books

An imprint of the Rowman & Littlefield Publishing Group, Inc.
Camden, Maine
www.downeastbooks.com

Distributed by National Book Network

Facing page: Fred A. Stone and David C. Montgomery are shown in their star-making roles as The Scarecrow and Tin Woodman in a poster for the 1902 stage musical of *The Wizard of Oz.*

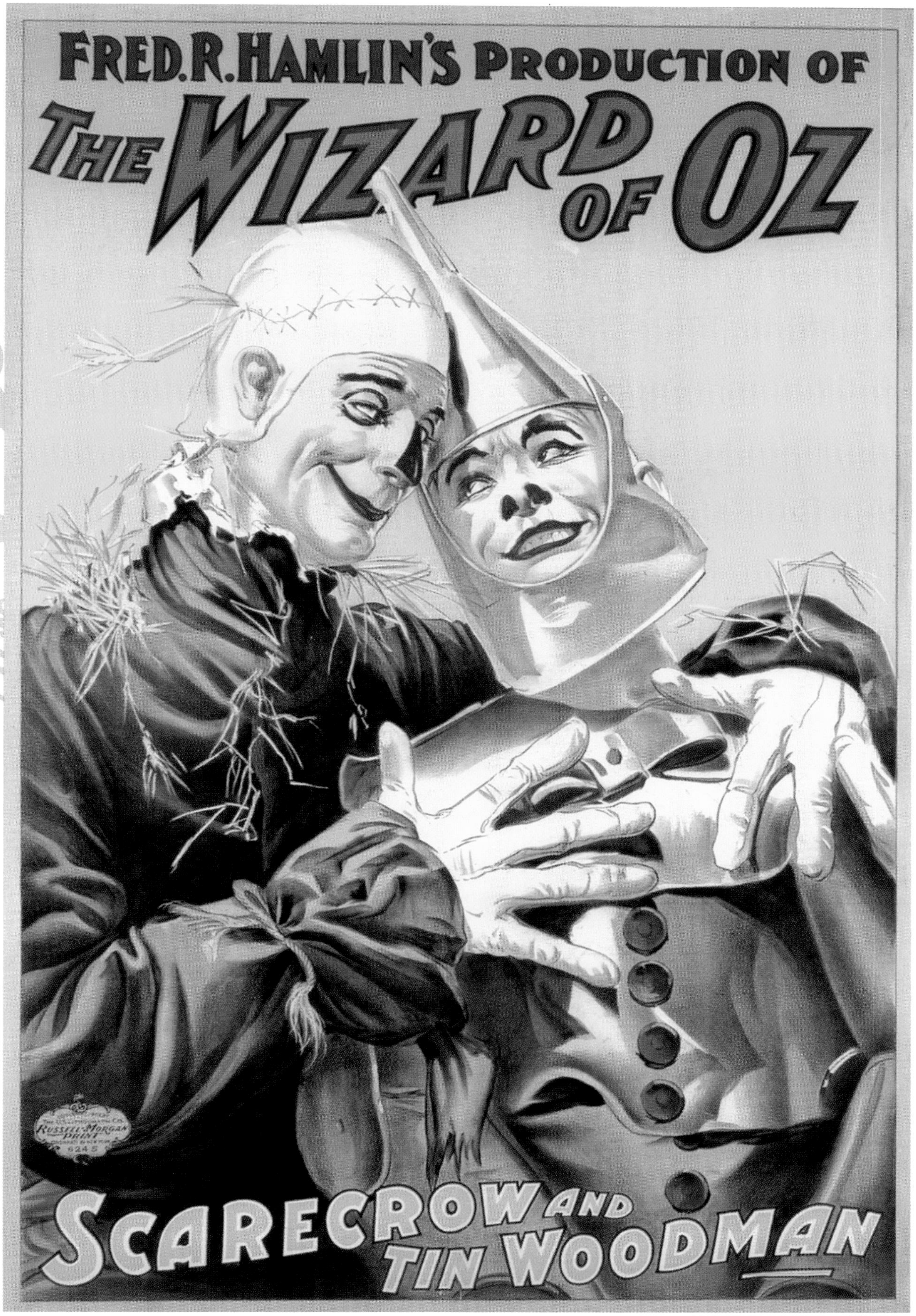
FRED. R. HAMLIN'S PRODUCTION OF
THE WIZARD OF OZ
SCARECROW AND TIN WOODMAN

CONTENTS~

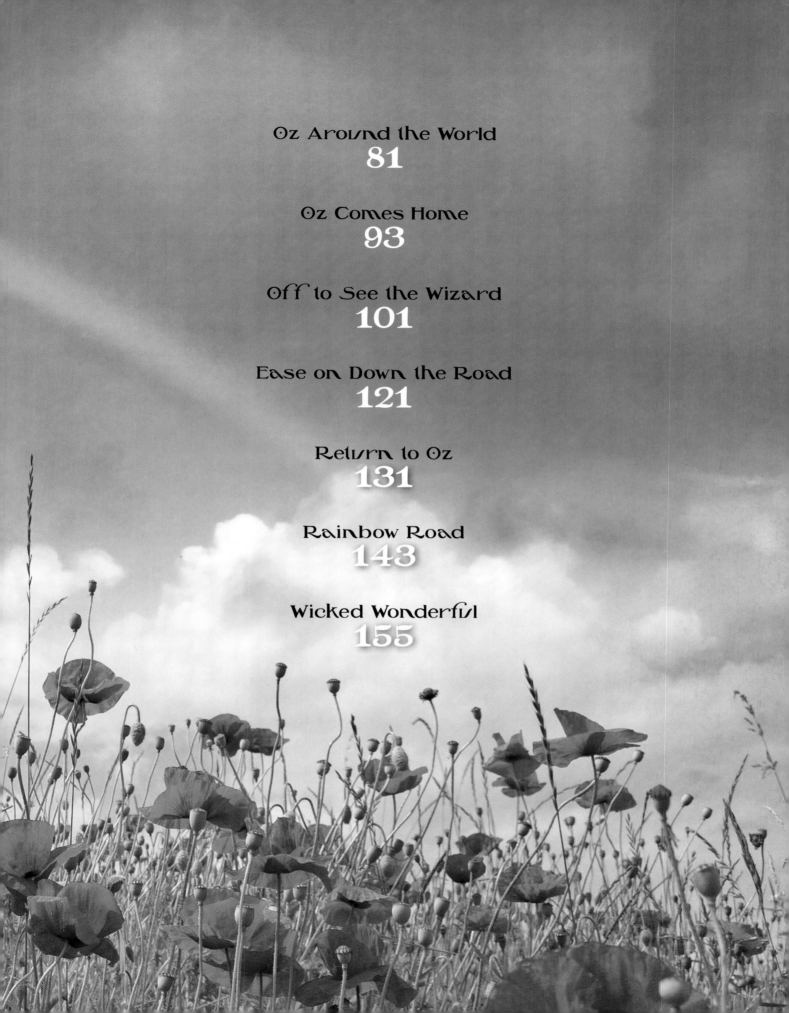

PREFACE

The Wonderful Wizard of Oz.

What is it about Oz, this story, the characters that compel us to return?

For me, the appeal goes beyond the MGM movie's "there's-no-place-like-home" philosophy. Resonant as that mantra is, as a child, I really couldn't get my head around why Dorothy would want to leave a land of color and go back to black-and-white.

In the first L. Frank Baum book, Dorothy actually goes to Oz — it's not a dream.

In later volumes she returns, ultimately making Oz her permanent home — trading upwards from a drab existence on the Kansas prairie to a phantasmagorical land of amazement and wonder and contentment.

No earthly MLS listing ever offered so much.

The Wizard of Oz is a book and movie propelled by magic and adventure and anchored in a search for identity.

The four main characters — Dorothy, the Scarecrow, the Tin Man, and the Cowardly Lion — already have within themselves what they are seeking. It takes time and effort and their collective and mutual support to realize their innate abilities.

The innocence and single-mindedness of a child focuses the fractured adults in their search and journey, so they can finally evolve into a wildly functional extended family.

Once they accept and embrace their strengths and gifts, they assume leadership in a community that celebrates the ultimate in creativity and diversity.

In Oz, flesh-and-bone creatures — both human and not-so-human — share space with men and women of tin and straw.

In Oz, matriarchs and patriarchs stand together to best serve their world.

In Oz, adults pay attention to the counsel of children.

More than 100 years since its first publication, the socially prescient nature of Baum's story now seems even more inspired. We may know how the story ends, but each revisiting reveals more.

More adventure.

More insight.

More serious fun.

The Wizard of Oz hints at the unknown promise of the future and provides solace and hope in the present.

And all the toys and games and stuff are pretty cool, too!

It all comes together in *The Wonderful World of Oz*.

~ **Willard Carroll** ~

C.I.A.
Judy
GARLAND
Frank
MORGAN
OZ
Regia:
VICTOR FLEMING
il MAGO di OZ
in TECHNICOLOR
PRODOTTO DA MERVYN LE ROY
ARTERO - ROMA

INTRODUCTION

Dorothy. The Yellow Brick Road. The Scarecrow, Tin Woodman, and Cowardly Lion. The Emerald City. Toto. The Wicked Witch of the West. The Poppy Field. The Munchkins. The Winged Monkeys. Glinda. In the history of American literature and entertainment, there are no better-known or more indelible images than these.

Brought to life with the publication of *The Wonderful Wizard of Oz* in 1900, the Land of Oz and its characters have long laid claim to an astounding fame. Now well into their second century of celebrity, they're sustained by a distinctive level of immeasurable, cross-generational love and familiarity. Indeed, it was authoritatively estimated as early as 1989 that it would be virtually impossible to find an American man or woman — or child over the age of two or three — who couldn't immediately identify a picture of Dorothy Gale and her friends.

There are many factors that led to such preeminence, but foremost among them are the imagination, heart, and communicative power of "Royal Historian" L. Frank Baum, his fellow Oz authors and illustrators — and the supremacy of the Metro-Goldwyn-Mayer motion picture studio in Hollywood's halcyon heyday. Other films, diverse stage productions, television showcases, home video releases, and mammoth merchandising would build on those foundations, additionally bolstering the audience for Baum's creations. Most recently (and almost unbelievably), public Ozzy passion somehow managed to hit new peaks of enthusiasm and international box office with the roaring success of the Broadway musical, *Wicked* (2003) and the "prequel" motion picture, *Oz the Great and Powerful* (2013). Both vehicles offered unassailable proof that the magic of Oz remains viable, self-renewing, and incomparable.

But Baum's talent for storytelling started it all. In turn, MGM created so compelling a screen version of his narrative in 1939 that, long

Above: A holiday sticker issued by W. L. Stensgaard & Associates, Inc., in conjunction with the Oz window displays they mounted under license from MGM (1939). **Facing page:** MGM's classic film didn't reach Italy until 1947 — after World War II. This is one of the rarer *Oz* film posters.

before its own 75th anniversary in 2014, it was exuberantly acknowledged as the most widely seen and quite possibly best-loved motion picture in history.

The prominence of the film and the impact of the latest theatrical and cinematic successes continue to obscure a greater Oz legend; the uninitiated invariably are surprised to learn that *The Wizard of Oz* (the adjective "Wonderful" was dropped from the title in 1903) was only the first of 40 official Oz books published between 1900 and 1963. Baum wrote 14; six other writers contributed the rest. From early on, Oz was promotionally touted — and eventually critically recognized — as "America's own fairyland," an appellation much in keeping with Baum's inspirations. Dorothy Gale of Kansas remains both timeless and a quintessential Midwestern child of 1900: sunny, brave, and

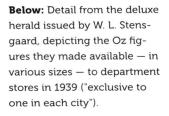

Below: Detail from the deluxe herald issued by W. L. Stensgaard, depicting the Oz figures they made available — in various sizes — to department stores in 1939 ("exclusive to one in each city").

resourceful, combining common sense with a capacity for friendship. Her companions had their origins in elements familiar to every youngster of the day; it was an era in which scarecrows reigned over cornfields, tin containers abounded on household shelves, lions could be seen in circuses (and a cowardly beast was an oxymoron to delight a child). Baum followed the same pattern for many of the curiosities he subsequently "discovered" in Oz — among them: Tik-Tok, a clock-work man who had to be wound like a timepiece to think, speak, and move; Jack Pumpkinhead, a carved and comic Halloween wonder; Scraps, a cotton-stuffed patchwork-quilt girl; the Woggle-Bug, a man-size, intellectually self-inflated insect; and a host of charming talking animals.

Similarly, Baum's fantasy devices aligned with or presupposed the century's industrial/mechanical age. (Tik-Tok may well have been literature's earliest robot.) Baum's books referenced flying "machines" or magical instruments that anticipated radio, television, electronic mail, and cellular phones. He regarded such magic as a science and was quick to assure his readers that the marvels wrought by sorcerers in Oz were no more miraculous than electricity and other discoveries effected by inventors in "the great outside world."

If Baum understood his approach, however, he did not much analyze it. At the onset of his career — years before Oz became central to his output — he stated his thesis; appropriately, it appeared in the introduction to *The Wizard*. While acknowledging that "the winged fairies of Grimm and Andersen have brought more happiness to childish hearts than all other human creations," Baum sought to move away from the "historical" European stories with their "fearsome moral to each tale. The time has come for a series of newer 'wonder tales'… Modern education includes morality; therefore the modern child seeks only entertainment in its wonder tales." *Oz*, he noted, "was written solely to pleasure children of today. It aspires to be a modernized fairy tale, in which the wonderment and joy are retained and the heartaches and nightmares are left out."

Thus, Baum was — from the beginning — writing for (but never down to) his audience, making Oz both identifiable and irresistible.

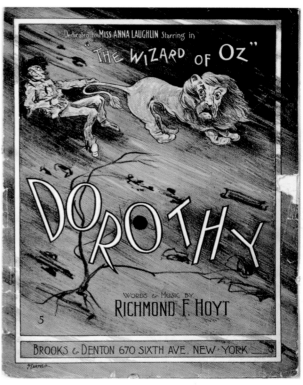

Above: Sheet music cover for a 1904 song "dedicated" to the actress who played Dorothy in the *Oz* stage show from 1902-1905. The song itself was not heard in the production.
Above left center: Engraved, collapsible metal cup and its souvenir box, presented to audience members in celebration of the 200th New York performance of *The Wizard of Oz* musical at the old Majestic Theatre, July 11, 1903.

M.DeLange présente

ZIGOTO dans

LE SORCIER D'OZ

ZIGOTO LE SORCIER D'OZ

LE FILM COMIQUE LE PLUS FANTASTIQUE

Above: French mini-poster for the 1925 Chadwick silent film version of *The Wizard of Oz*. "Zigoto" was the name by which "Scarecrow" Larry Semon was known to Gallic audiences.

And despite the prior assertion, his new American fairy tales heartily embraced a certain amount of heartache and nightmare; children reveled in it, perhaps because his wicked witches and winged monkeys were always fortuitously overcome.

The Baum Oz stories did, however, manage to eliminate most intimations of romance, a topic not as germane to his youthful readers as adventure and quest. (On the two occasions a courtship concept infiltrated his books, it originated in a musical comedy script and a motion picture scenario only later adapted for use as Oz plots.) But Ruth Plumly Thompson, Baum's successor as "Royal Historian of Oz" from 1921-1939, had no such compunction; at least six of her 19 titles took delight in partnering princes, princesses, and lesser royalty. It was an indication that Oz had moved with the times, as contemporary movies, radio, novels, and magazines wallowed in the romantic trenches as well.

Such variation fazed no readers. By 1960, when the Oz series was all but complete, its publishers took promotional pride when they could note that, "In a recent survey, *The New York Times* polled a group of teenagers on the books they liked best when they were young. The Oz books topped the list." The claim is not surprising; millions of volumes had by then found their way into print, and that figure has since easily doubled itself. There have been hundreds of versions of *The Wizard of Oz* alone, whether full-text, adaptation, or abridgement; all 39 sequels have gone through multiple printings as well. Since 1932–1933, when the first two Baum titles appeared in France, Oz has also become an increasing presence in children's literature in scores of foreign languages.

Above: Box cover for Oz note-paper issued by White & Wyckoff (1925). Each piece was embellished by John R. Neill or W. W. Denslow artwork from the Oz books.

The Oz books comprise the cornerstone of countless collections, but there has been limitless subsidiary merchandising as well. (Though not the norm in 1900, massive exploitation grew with the recognition and diversification of Oz, and related products became prime examples of the twentieth century's ever-increasing commercialization.) The present-day competition to accumulate Oz material is especially intense as it has become an integral element in several collectible forums: Americana, fantasy, motion picture history, and as a key ingredient in the career of MGM's "Dorothy," Judy Garland. Even throwaway promotional items are now valuable to thousands of devotees.

The success of Oz also ran parallel to the development of the century's media. The fame of the first book was expanded by an outrageously popular stage play in 1902, which in turn propelled the demand for additional stories. Their fame was enlarged by the 1939 MGM film, which received its greater glory by becoming a traditional television event beginning in 1956. Such omnipresence was further amplified when home video meant the movie could be viewed at will; that specific accessibility made it possible for happy obsession and virtual memorization by new devotees, many of them enraptured preschoolers.

Even its most fervent partisans, however, were genuinely astounded at the manner in which Oz surged into the twenty-first century. All past praise was renewed; many new levels of presentation and interpretation were extolled. The expansive power of Oz was heightened by technical and scientific innovations that Baum himself would have appreciated. Internet research and dialogue flew around the world, collecting-from-home became a norm, and social networking evolved into its own Yellow Brick Road for countless fans.

New millennium interest in Oz additionally was propelled by

Above: Early in the twentieth century, L. Frank Baum boasted that there already were foreign editions of his Oz books. But the first known translation didn't appear until 1932 when *The Wizard of Oz* was published in France.

renewed levels of enthusiasm for reading and fantasy in general. J. K. Rowling's seven volumes about boy wizard Harry Potter saw publication between 1997 and 2007 and evolved into an eight-film series. Peter Jackson brought J. R. R. Tolkien's *The Lord of the Rings* trilogy to the screen between 2001 and 2003; there were also movie adaptations of three of the C. S. Lewis *Chronicles of Narnia*. Amidst such make-believe, Oz — even more so than these (or Alice's Wonderland or Peter Pan's Never Land) — was a supremely comfortable destination. Its intrigue and capacity to delight were further heightened by its age-old, matter-of-fact alchemy and firm footing in America-related protagonists and values.

As a result, the widespread influence of Oz to date now would be impossible to chart. The word itself has passed into common usage to denote a beautiful or unusual location. (Its emergence as the name of a security prison in a 1990s cable television series falls into the latter classification.) "Munchkin" designates anything diminutive. The green landscape of Seattle has won it the nickname "Emerald City." Commercial products from soap to medication have utilized Oz personalities as their sales force. Situations from *The Wizard of Oz* have been parodied in periodicals and television programs and adapted for video games, cookbooks, window displays, flower and fashion shows, and anti-drug and AIDS-awareness dramas. Oz has provided concepts and characters for political cartoons dating back to William Randolph Hearst, discrediting or humorizing dozens of governmental administrations. In 1959, "Project Ozma" was established at the West Virginia National Radio Astronomy laboratory to monitor possible signals from outer space; it took its name from the benevolent princess who arrived to rule Oz after the Wizard's departure. By the 1990s, TOTO — or Transportable Tornado Observatory — was a mainstay of the National Weather Service, designed to measure wind and air pressure in violent storms.

Allusions to the MGM film continue to season dozens of other motion pictures, conspicuously *E.T.* and *Star Wars*, whose themes and images paid unquestioned homage while maintaining their own integrity. Oz references have also permeated pop songs, and an Oz-association can provide mountains of publicity; witness the stir caused when Pink Floyd's *Dark Side of the Moon* album was rumored to "fit" as an alternate soundtrack to portions of the 1939 movie. The same kind of speculation has led dark-minded individuals to conjure a visible, hanging, on-set Munchkin corpse out of what is merely an oversized, wing-flapping bird in a sequence of the same film.

Over the years, Baum and Oz have influenced (or found advocates in) authors from James Thurber, Ellery Queen, Ray Bradbury, and Harlan Ellison to Gore Vidal. Even Salman Rushdie has rhapsodized about the effect the *Oz* film had on him as a child in Bombay. The greater Oz legend also inspired new, adult-themed books, including Geoff Ryman's *Was* and Gregory Maguire's *Wicked* — the latter a precursor to the musical of the same title. Roger Baum, great-grandson of L. Frank, has carried on family tradition in a dozen of his own Oz stories for children.

Such monumental impact has not grown unchallenged. Early-to-mid-twentieth century authorities and critics complained that Oz books fell short of standard literary criteria: style, plot, characterization, and theme. But as Dr. C. Warren Hollister pointed out in 1970, the series overcame such objections on its own terms; he added a fifth criterion which the Oz books possessed to a prodigious degree — "three-dimensionality." In his words, such an attribute afforded readers the chance to "enter the adventure [and] actually travel…into Oz."

Renown, familiarity, and controversy have also engendered "interpretations" of Oz, Baum, the stories, and the film. Books draw conclusions *From Confucius to Oz* and consider *The Zen of Oz.* There have been Marxist, Communist, Biblical, sexual, and spiritual "clarifications" — and fundamentalist objections. (Per some religious conservatives, there can be no such thing as a good witch.) Essayists have addressed feminism, Freudian explications, and the matriarchy of the land. Dorothy has been psychoanalyzed in her role as an orphan; the Good and Wicked Witches of Oz have been made to represent different facets of Aunt Em or decoded as symbols of the Good and Bad Mother who "deserted" Dorothy in the first place. The Kansas girl herself is not merely surrounded by such ruling forces for good as fairy princess Ozma and beneficent sorceress Glinda but encumbered by "deficient" males who hide their humbuggery, or search for brains, heart, and courage.

The most prevalent interpretation of Baum's first Oz story defines it as a parable of the Populist movement, a theory initially put

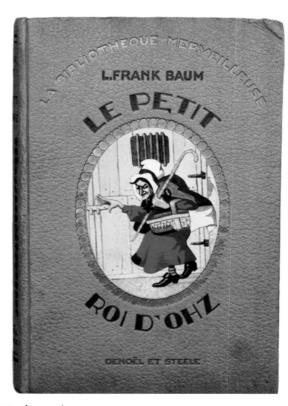

Above: France followed its initial Oz title with a translation of Baum's first sequel, *The Marvelous Land of Oz* (1933).

forth as little more than casual coincidence by a high school teacher in the early 1960s. His concept, published in *American Quarterly* (Spring 1964), was almost immediately pounced upon by academicians who knew little about Baum and less about his writings; it has since been so widely circulated as to be foolishly reported and taught as fact. In truth, there's every indication that *Oz* first emerged as an installment-upon-installment, evening-after-evening, told-aloud fantasy devised by its author to enthrall an audience of children — a reality since stressed by premier Baum scholar/historian Michael Patrick Hearn and all surviving members of the Baum family. (A particularly potent dismissal of the Populist connection came when it was offered that Baum's widow, sons, or succeeding heirs would have leapt to embrace such a "meaningful" association during the early-to-mid-twentieth century when *Oz* was routinely, cavalierly diminished by historians and critics of children's literature — or banned by librarians.) When recently asked to interview an averred exponent of the Populist theory, a *Chicago Sun-Times* reporter came away recollecting another college professor, Baum's Woggle-Bug, "an over-educated insect."

Not surprisingly, there have been many more affirmative than negative assessments of the virtues of Oz; Baum's kingdom has been most realistically recognized as Utopia. In *The Georgia Review* (Fall 1960), S.J. Sackett listed the lightly incorporated lessons to be learned from the series and noted, "The[se] attitudes…are all positive ones, and among them you can find practically the complete roll call of the attitudes desirable to insure the continuance of democracy, of civilization, of life…."

Given the enduring, all-ages appeal and

Below: *The Wizard of Oz Abroad.* The 1957 Italian *Il Mago di Oz* boasted stunning illustrations by Maraja — so much so that an English version of the same edition was published in the United States a year later.

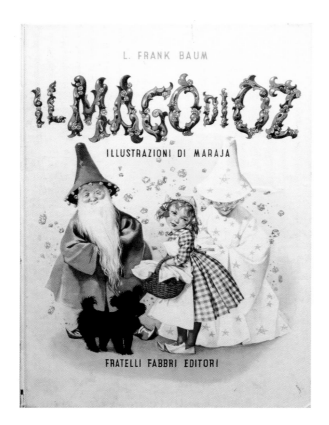

potency of Oz, however, it may be most fair to delineate its philosophies as simply as possible. On an Ozian excursion, one encounters again and again a gentle propaganda in both overt expressions of individuality and demonstrations of loyalty and courage. Its myths are lodged in the message that good triumphs over evil, and while this may hardly provide an all-encompassing preparation for adulthood, it remains an ideology to seek and support. (It also gives children, however briefly, the carefree-dom to be children, an increasingly abandoned custom in the literature and entertainment often offered on their behalf.)

Finally, *The Wizard of Oz* correlates to the life journey of every individual. This may well be the primary reason the story has so successfully traveled the world, despite its many American components. Dorothy is Everychild, and children immediately relate to her adventures. Any girl or boy can identify with the terror of being lost and the desire to return home, or — as per the film — the fear of losing a cherished pet, or the need to escape family on occasion. A teenager can parallel (whether consciously or not) the self-doubts of Dorothy's companions: Am I smart? Am I brave? Am I capable of loving

Above: As proud sponsors of the 1966 CBS telecast of MGM's *The Wizard of Oz*, Proctor & Gamble gave away plastic hand-puppet "premiums," attached to several of their soap products.

and being loved? Finally, an adult comes to a perception perhaps best summarized by MGM "Scarecrow" Ray Bolger: "Everyone has a brain, everyone has a heart, everyone has courage. These are the gifts given to people on earth, and if you use them properly, they lead you home. And home isn't a house or an abode, it's people — people you love and people who love you. That's a home." (Those who would degrade the "no-place-like-home" motif bypass Bolger's point: Dorothy's home was the correct one for her at that particular time. As years passed, locale and family members would vary for her — and for everyone. The quest for love and "home" would not.)

But whatever the reasons for its mass appeal, the world of Oz was conceived, designed, and realized as pure entertainment, and it has maintained that signature quality in all of its successful incarnations across more than eleven decades. (Given Baum's past guises as theatrical showman and pioneer film-maker, he doubtless would revel in the powerful reactions aroused by *Wicked* and *Oz the Great and Powerful*; despite their alterations and purposeful ignorance of the Royal Historian's own accounts, both are founded in his emotions and spirit.) The history and greater Oz legend as presented in these pages is meant as entertainment, as well: a celebratory memory book and pictorial overview of the contributions of Oz to our jubilant emotions.

Many deserve credit for all the things Oz has come to represent: authors and illustrators, publishers and entrepreneurs, Judy Garland and MGM. But Frank Baum generated it — out of a blessed compassion for children, a desire to divert, and a quiet, informal mission to inspire hearts, souls, and imaginations. In a presentation copy of *Mother Goose In Prose* (1897), Baum wrote to his sister: "When I was young, I longed to write a great novel that should win me fame. Now that I am getting old, my first book is written to amuse children. For, aside from my evident inability to do anything 'great,' I have learned to regard fame as a will-o'-the-wisp which, when caught, is not worth the possession; but to please a child is a sweet and lovely thing that warms one's heart and brings its own reward...."

Baum's implementation of that ideal resulted in a canon of transcendent joy. The number of lives he and his universe have gladdened and gratified may well be unsurpassed by the similar achievements of anyone else — and it's the purity of his underlying, happy emotion that continues to give the wonderful world of Oz its pervasive power.

THEY'RE BACK!

ALL THE WONDERFUL WIZARD OF OZ BOOKS

by L. Frank Baum
with the Original Illustrations
by W. W. Denslow & John R. Neill

Above: Reilly & Lee, the Oz book publishers, had artist/aficionado Dick Martin design new covers for the 14 Baum titles in 1964. This poster heralds the sturdy, refashioned reprints.

DOWN the YELLOW BRICK ROAD

When *The Wonderful Wizard of Oz* appeared in 1900, 44-year-old L. Frank Baum was the veteran of a dozen careers — actor, playwright, storekeeper, newspaperman, and traveling salesman among them. Though blessed with intelligence, wit, charm, and presence, he'd achieved only sporadic financial stability. By 1897, with a family to support, he was living in Chicago as the editor of a magazine that encouraged innovative display advertising in department store windows. It was this settled existence, however — and a burgeoning association with local writers and artists — that led to the publication of his first children's book, *Mother Goose In Prose* (1897). Comprised of stories Baum had originally devised as verbal entertainment for his four sons and their friends, the volume boasted illustrations by Maxfield Parrish and ultimately proved to be more an artistic than financial triumph. But Baum had finally found a vocation; it would quickly bring him a success he'd never imagined, an imperishable fame — and lead directly to the Emerald City.

His next effort, *Father Goose: His Book* (1899), was a best-selling compilation of nonsense verse for children, prodigiously enhanced by the illustrations of W.W. Denslow. But the real miracle struck as the century turned: among the five Baum titles published in 1900, preeminent even then was *The Wonderful Wizard of Oz*. *The New York Times* found it "bright and joyous" and omnisciently offered, "It will indeed be strange if there be a normal child who will not enjoy the story." The first edition was a picturesque novelty with its 24 color plates and many line drawings; Denslow's conceptions of the characters and landscapes contributed immeasurably to the book's popularity.

Top and above: L. Frank Baum's napkin ring (engraved "Frank") and his letterhead, the latter designed by W. W. Denslow at the time of *Father Goose: His Book* (1899). Born Lyman Frank Baum in Chittenango, NY, on May 15, 1856, the author disliked and seldom used his first name. **Facing page:** L. Frank Baum and The Oz Books.

Above: Labels for products manufactured by the Baum family in New York State in the 1880s. Baum pursued multiple professions before settling into his writing career in the late 1890s.

Baum wrote five additional fantasies in the next three years, but the happy die had already, unwittingly been cast. The success of *Oz* led to its adaptation as a lavish stage extravaganza, produced in Chicago in 1902 prior to a Broadway debut the following January. New York reviews were mixed, but so potent was the power of Baum's creations that the show became an extraordinary hit. One major manifestation of its appeal was the "blizzard of Oz" mail from children who saw the play and/or read the book; all clamored for "more about Oz" from its author. (Unlike the later MGM film treatment, the original Oz story did not present Dorothy's adventures as a dream. The virtual reality of Baum's narrative meant that a sequel was indeed imaginable.)

To answer the requests — and provide himself with the foundation for what he hoped would be another lucrative musical comedy — Baum wrote *The Marvelous Land Of Oz* (1904). He and Denslow had fallen out over the division of royalties from the stage *Wizard*, so illustrations for the new title (and all of Baum's subsequent Oz books) were done by John R. Neill. A young Philadelphian, Neill possessed a sweeping flair and whimsicality that brought Oz even more vividly to life.

Baum promoted the new Oz title through a newspaper cartoon series, "Queer Visitors from the Marvelous Land Of Oz" (1904-1905) and *The Woggle-Bug Book* (1905). His subsequent 1905 stage musical was also titled *The Woggle-Bug* (after a new character in *The Marvelous Land…*), but the show was a quick failure.

Nonetheless, Baum persevered; in fact, his literary output for 1905-1907 also included three full-length fantasies and 15 short stories for children, four novels for adults, and five books for teenagers (the latter just the onset of two dozen "series" titles in all, most of them published under a variety of pseudonyms). No matter how adroit the work, however, he was beset by pleas for "more about Oz" and its Kansas protagonist.

So, Dorothy returned in *Ozma of Oz* (1907), as she did the following year — with another familiar friend — in *Dorothy and the Wizard in Oz*. *The Road to Oz* (1909) continued the pattern; each title was received with enthusiasm by critics and rapture by readers.

Such a ready audience also turned out to see Baum "in person" when he briefly toured in the critically-acclaimed

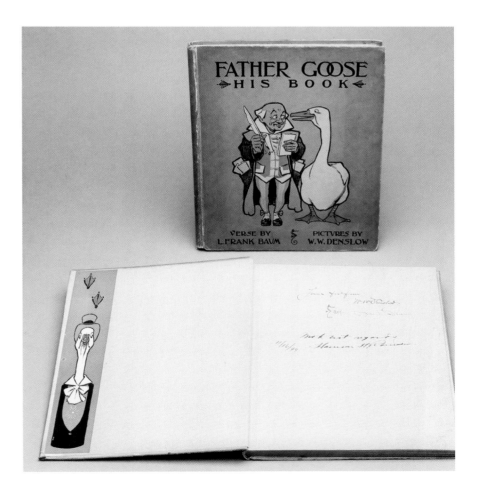

Above: The cover of the songbook issued in conjunction with Baum's touring stage musical, *The Maid of Arran* (1882). He wrote the script, music, and lyrics, and starred in the show. **Left:** This copy of *Father Goose: His Book* (1899) includes a flyleaf inscription from Baum, Denslow, and friend and business associate Harrison Rountree.

Above: Denslow's 1900 book poster for the three titles he and Baum had thus far produced together. **Right:** The first edition of *The Wonderful Wizard of Oz* (Chicago: The George M. Hill Company, 1900; Bobbs-Merrill took over publication of the book in 1903).

Fairylogue and Radio-Plays (1908). A combination of lecture, live orchestra, slide illustrations, and hand-colored film clips, his presentation drew from the plots of the first three Oz novels but quickly came in off the road as too expensive to sustain itself. Baum was never a businessman, and his heavy personal investment in the creation of the production eventually, severely damaged his financial security.

By 1910 — and for all the unconditional success of the Oz books themselves — Baum decided to invest his future talents in "other stories" and publicly declared he would end the series with *The Emerald City of Oz.* His plot brought Dorothy, Aunt Em, Uncle Henry, and Toto to Oz as permanent residents and culminated in a magic spell (cast by Glinda the Good) that rendered the entire country invisible to any but the eyes of its own citizens. Baum's penultimate paragraph quoted the poignant note of farewell he "received" from his heroine:

You will never hear anything more about Oz, because we are now cut off forever from all the rest of the world. But Toto and I will always love you and all the other children who love us.

— DOROTHY GALE

Above: An extraordinary 1903 lithographed poster for *The Wizard of Oz* stage musical. Throughout the seven-season tour of the show by multiple companies, the Poppy Field scene was a highlight. Good Witch Locasta (center, near top) saved Dorothy and her friends from the poisonous flowers by invoking a blizzard. Also shown are new characters: Pastoria (rightful ruler of Oz), Tryxie Tryfle (his fiancée from Kansas), and Dorothy's pet cow, Imogene. (Toto didn't appear in the stage show.)

Right: Dorothy (Anna Laughlin) and Imogene (Edwin J. Stone) discover The Scarecrow (Fred A. Stone). In real life, The Scarecrow and cow were brothers.

26

Above: The act one finale, wherein the Snow Queen saves Dorothy & Company by freezing the poppies. **Left:** Act three of the diverse plotting saw the Tin Woodman briefly caged upstage, while the Scarecrow held forth front and center. (Prints of all three production photos were made from the original 1903 glass slides.)

Right: This lithographed poster (circa 1903) shows David C. Montgomery as the stage musical Tin Woodman. Originally slotted for a minor role in the show, Montgomery — and vaudeville partner Fred A. Stone, who'd been cast as the Scarecrow — ultimately insisted on his appearing as the Tin Man so they could "play together" throughout. **Above:** This paperback gag book was an unauthorized "tie-in" to the production (1904).

Left: 1903 lithographed poster. For thousands of theatergoers and more than three decades of entertainment history, Stone remained the Scarecrow of fond memory. As late as 1939, noted critic Burns Mantle regretted that the then-66-year-old Stone had not been cast to re-create his performance in the MGM film. **Below:** Souvenir photograph (1903) and hand-colored postcard (1904) of Stone's Scarecrow. **Center bottom:** Self-caricature of the character, drawn by Stone decades after he first assayed the role.

FROM·KANSAS·LITTLE·DOROTHY·TO·OZ·WAS·BLOWN·AWAY;
WHERE·FIRST·SHE·MET·THE·GAY·SCARECROW;·THE·MAN·ALL·STUFFED·WITH·HAY·
IMOGENE;·THE·SPOTTED·CALF,·WAS·GLAD·TO·SEE·HIM;·TOO,
AND·TRIED·AT·ONCE·TO·EAT·HIM·UP·WHICH·SCARED·HIM·THROUGH·AND·THROUGH.

THE·TIN·MAN·IN·A·SHOWER·OF·RAIN·GOT·RUST·IN·EVERY·JOINT,
SO·HE·MUST·CARRY·AN·OIL·CAN·HIS·ELBOWS·TO·ANOINT·
NEXT·CAME·A·LION·COWARDLY,·AS·TIMID·AS·A·BIRD;
YET·IF·SOME·DANGER·THREATENED·DOT·HIS·MIGHTY·ROAR·WAS·HEARD.

THE·WICKED·WITCH·THE·MOTOR·MAN·AND·TRIXY·SWEET·AS·HONEY,
GABRIEL·THE·POET·BOY·ALL·THOUGHT·THE·SCARECROW·FUNNY·
FOR·HE·AND·DOT·AND·TIN·MAN·TOO·DANCED·ALL·A·MERRY·MEASURE·
TO·PLEASE·THE·PEOPLE·ONE·AND·ALL·AND·GIVE·THE·WIZARD·PLEASURE

THE LION WISHED THAT HE WERE BRAVE, THE SCARECROW WANTED BRAINS,
THE TIN MAN CRAVED A LOVING HEART WITH ALL ITS JOYS AND PAINS
FAIR DOROTHY WOULD FAIN GO BACK TO KANSAS AND HER FOLKS
ALTHOUGH SHE LIKED THE TIN MAN AND THE SCARECROW'S JOLLY JOKES.

SO TO THE CITY EMERALD, IN SPITE OF WITCH AND BLIZZARD,
THIS FUNNY CREW TRAMPED MILES AND MILES, TO SEE THE MIGHTY WIZARD
WHEN THEY GOT THERE THEY FOUND IT FULL OF FUNNY KINDS OF FOLK.
CAP RISKIT, LADY LUNATIC, THE ARMY WAS A JOKE.

TWAS THUS, THE FOUR ALL GOT THEIR WISH; HIS HEART THE TIN MAN GOT,
THE SCARECROW HAD HIS BRAINS; AND HOME WENT LITTLE DOT.
BUT TWAS GOLINDA, GENTLE QUEEN, THAT HELPED HER SO, I THINK
AND SENT HER TO HER KANSAS HOME AS QUICK AS YOU COULD WINK.

Prior spread: Six nursery-room wallpaper panels offer a frieze of Denslow-drawn personalities and incidents from the *Wizard* stage musical. He depicts several comic characters added to the show for adult entertainment appeal by director Julian Mitchell, including Captain Riskit, the Lady Lunatic, and Gabriel the Poet Boy (love interest for Dorothy). Not all of them appeared in the actual production under those names (nor did a Wicked Witch or "Golinda"), which suggests that the accompanying rhymes may have been based on alternate script concepts. **Right:** Denslow book poster (1904). After the dissolution of his partnership with Baum, the artist illustrated and wrote other children's stories, several of which featured Oz characters. **Below:** Nine of Baum's non-Oz fantasy books for children, 1897-1906.

ST NICHOLAS
1905 FOR YOUNG FOLKS 1905

A Serial Story, "Queen Zixi of Ix"
By L. Frank Baum, Author of
"THE WIZARD OF OZ"
Superbly Illustrated in Color

Top: Front, side, top, and bottom "Oz panels" from a box of candy sold across the years during performances of the 1902 stage production. **Above:** A 1907 letter from the manager of the Lyceum Theatre announces the coming engagement of *The Wizard of Oz*. **Left:** A 1909 newspaper serialization of *The Wizard of Oz*. **Far left:** Book poster for Baum's personal favorite of his output. *Queen Zixi of Ix* (1905) was serialized monthly in the *St. Nicholas* magazine before its hardcover publication.

Above: Sheet music cover art for Baum's 1905 musical, *The Woggle-Bug*. **Top:** Perhaps the first Oz "toy" was this Parker Brothers box of riddle-cards, linked to Baum's overgrown insect but with no other Oz connection (circa 1905). **Above right:** One of Baum's "Queer Visitors..." stories, syndicated in newspapers for 26 weeks during 1904-05. The series was illustrated by contemporary political cartoonist Walt McDougall. **Right:** "Woggle-Bug Lessons" cards, adapted at the time from McDougall's drawings. **Facing page bottom:** Baum with the cast of his multi-media *Fairy-Logue and Radio Plays* (1908), which included the very first Oz motion pictures. Two years later, Oz came to the screen again via three one-reel films from the Selig Polyscope Company. **Facing page top:** Sign posters relax in front of their billboard heralding the *Radio Plays*.

35

Above: Baum's *Juvenile Speaker* (1910) collected excerpts from his earlier work; *The Sea Fairies* (1911) and *Sky Island* (1912) marked his attempt to escape from Oz. By 1913, a promotional splash for *The Patchwork Girl of Oz* and the "Little Wizard Series" proclaimed his return.

The Royal Historian of Oz

The onset of the decade marked a fresh start for Baum. He and his wife relocated to a peaceful Los Angeles suburb called Hollywood and affectionately christened their home "Ozcot." He had plans for new musical shows, and the "other stories" he hoped to tell were launched in two superlative fantasies, *The Sea Fairies* (1911) and *Sky Island* (1912).

But reality set in quickly. The books failed to sell, and Baum was additionally burdened by a pile of old debts, many incurred on behalf of the *Radio-Plays.* In 1911, he was forced to file for bankruptcy (or, as one of the more sardonic headlines put it, "L. Frank Baum is 'Broke,' He Says"). To satisfy creditors, Baum signed over future royalties on several of his early children's fantasies, including *The Wizard of Oz.*

There was, however, a saving reality as well: the magic of Oz not only lingered but thrived. Baum had always demonstrated an unsurpassed ability to bring his characters to life. They now returned the favor by continuing to flourish, even though his attentions had been elsewhere. By 1912, the author's future was in their hands: the Oz books had independently maintained their prodigious popularity, and Baum re-embraced his kingdom with happy, appreciative vigor.

Appropriately enough, the link required to reconnect with an invisible fairyland was provided by the powers of imagination he had unconsciously cultivated in his "Ozzy" readers. In *The Patchwork Girl of Oz* (the 1913 "comeback" volume), Baum explained: "One of the children inquired why we couldn't hear from…Dorothy by wireless telegraph." Thus, the magical barrier was pierced, communication was reestablished with the Emerald City, and the latest news from Oz could again be shared.

To help relaunch and republicize the series, Baum wrote six booklets about his most famous characters; a year later, those tales were reassembled in a single volume as *Little Wizard Stories of Oz* (1914).

L. FRANK BAUM telling "OZ" stories at Coronado

Top: Baum entrances his adherents in Coronado, CA, where he wintered and wrote for several years. **Above:** Sheet music for *The Tik-Tok Man of Oz* stage show (1913).

Below: A toy top and celluloid pin helped to promote the new Oz book for 1915.

He also revised an earlier, unproduced musical comedy libretto, which Oliver Morosco presented with success on the West Coast and on tour as *The Tik-Tok Man of Oz* (1913). Though the show never made it to New York, its excellent score, worthy cast, and opulent scenic effects provided a satisfactory theatrical experience for all ages.

Baum's annual Oz book was by now a happy inevitability, but he fell creatively prey to his new environment as well. The motion picture industry was growing up around him, and in 1914, he founded The Oz Film Manufacturing Company. His partners were fellow members of The Uplifters, a Los Angeles-based businessmen's organization; together, they established their own studio and, within months, Baum had overseen three five-reel features based on his fantasies. But Oz Films encountered distribution problems and (once those were resolved) audience antipathy for what was dismissed as "children's entertainment." Two scripts fashioned for adults were quickly placed into production, but the company was soon thereafter dissolved.

Scarecrow

Tin woodman

Jack Pumpkinhead

Above: Three of John R. Neill's 54 cutout characters, drawn by the inimitable artist for *The Oz Toy Book.* Even though the board-bound collection was intended as short-term promotion for the Oz series, Baum was not consulted about its publication, and the author was unhappily astounded when he saw the work advertised in Reilly & Lee's 1915 catalogue. Today, few of the fragile *Toy* books survive intact or complete.

Above: Cover art for *The Oz Toy Book* (1915). **Below:** The Woozy — a separately distributed, promotional cutout toy of a new character from *The Patchwork Girl of Oz* book and film (1913 and 1914, respectively).

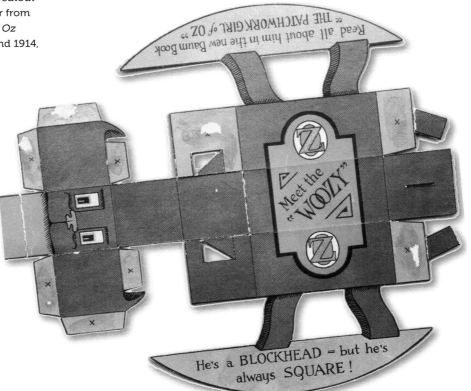

Baum had no money in the firm, so its failure had no financial impact on him; he continued to write and enjoy life in Southern California. He often socialized with other Uplifters, annually contributing material to and performing in their informal theatricals. An expert (if amateur) horticulturist, he won nearly two dozen cups for the prize dahlias and chrysanthemums he grew at Ozcot. Such physical activity — along with golf or a quiet walk through the neighborhood — gave Baum time to mentally evolve the plots of his new stories before committing them to paper. Sixty years later, veteran Hollywood journalist/scenarist Adela Rogers St. Johns remembered his "extraordinary twinkle of *joie de vivre*" at such times: "I used to meet him taking a little soul-and-back stretching stroll down Bronson Avenue to Hollywood Boulevard…as he companioned no doubt with the Scarecrow and the Tin Woodman and the Cowardly Lion, and of course, Dorothy." Perhaps one of Baum's greatest delights came in meeting with his young fans; the Oz books were beginning to attract their second generations of readers.

By 1917, however, his health was failing. Plagued with a weak heart since childhood, Baum suffered angina attacks and then gall bladder and appendix trouble. Subsequent surgery left him an invalid, although he continued to write of Oz and dictate responses to letters from "his" children as long as he could.

On May 6, 1919, the "Royal Historian" died at Ozcot. According to family legend, he spoke his last semi-conscious words to his wife, drifting away after a quiet reference to the deadly desert one had to traverse to reach the Land of Oz: "Now we can cross the shifting sands.…"

Below: Advertising herald for The Oz Film Manufacturing Company's silent feature, *The New Wizard of Oz* (1915).
Below left: Baum's personal bookplate, referencing the new home he and wife Maud built in California.

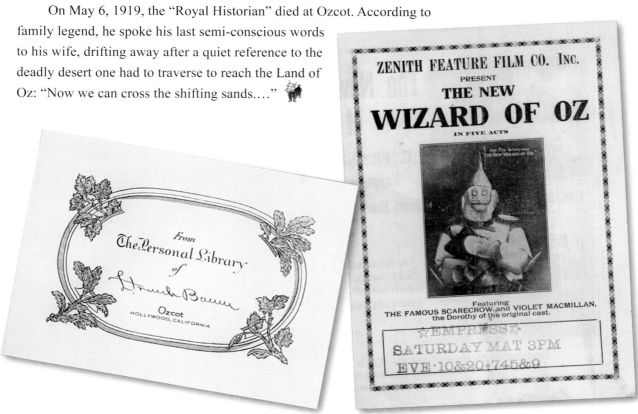

Right: Officers of The Oz Film Manufacturing Company (1914-1915). From left: Secretary Clarence Rundel, President Baum, Treasurer H. M. Haldeman, and Vice President Louis F. Gottschalk (who also scored music to accompany the silent films).

Below: Interior of ad flyer for *The Last Egyptian,* adapted for the screen from Baum's adult novel which had been published anonymously in 1908.

THE LAST EGYPTIAN

A SPECTACULAR ROMANCE OF THE ORIENT
Featuring J. FARRELL McDONALD and VIVIAN REED
SUPPORTED BY A STAR CAST

OZ FILMS
The Oz Film Manufacturing Company
Santa Monica Boulevard; Gower to Lodi Streets
LOS ANGELES,   **CALIFORNIA**

NEW YORK OFFICE   220 WEST 42nd STREET
Frank J. Baum   *Special Representative*

L. FRANK BAUM
Famous "Wizard of Oz" man whose books and plays have been enjoyed by millions of people

Mr. L. Frank Baum

L. Frank Baum, the president and general manager of the Oz Film Manufacturing Company of Los Angeles, is famous the world over for his quaint books and the extraordinary characters he has invented.

Mr. Baum has written and published twenty-six successful books; of the number are more successful children's books than are credited to any other author. Of these, the ten Oz books have sold over four million copies during the last six years. They are translated in nearly all languages and have almost as large a sale in Great Britain and Germany as in this country.

Believing that there was a field for a new line of motion picture plays, Mr. Baum organized the Oz Film Manufacturing Company last spring. The first production was "The Patchwork Girl of Oz," a photo-extravaganza full of genuine comedy, quaint characters and pretty girls. The work is all done under Mr. Baum's personal direction and supervision, and he has shown a capacity for making just as successful motion pictures as he did books and musical shows.
—*Moving Picture World.*

VIOLET MacMILLAN
"The Daintiest Darling of them all"

She plays leads with the Oz Film Manufacturing Co.

Violet Macmillan first become prominent when she appeared in the leading role of "Dorothy" in the "Wizard of Oz" Company organized by Hurtig & Seamon. She was by far the most successful actress who ever essayed this part.

She was the original girl in "The Time, The Place, and The Girl," and has been identified with musical comedy for a number of years.

During the past year she was a headliner on the Orpheum circuit, when she was called "The Modern Cinderella" on account of her tiny feet and perfect figure. Miss Macmillan is full of personality and her countenance is so bright and vivacious that she instantly wins all hearts.

"THE PATCHWORK GIRL OF OZ"
An appreciation by the Rev. W. H. Jackson in the Moving Picture World of October 17, 1914

Advertisements are too often exaggerating and lead to disappointment, when the vaunted ideals are not realized. Fortunately this does not apply to the "Patchwork Girl of Oz"; if anything its merits are under rather than over-advertised, giving one that pleasure of realizing something beyond expectations. "It is better than we expected," is the best advertisement any picture can receive, besides paying the highest compliment to those producing it. Without doubt this was the general tenor of the sentiment of a large audience in a leading New York theater during the first week of this picture.

For several years we have had so much foolishness labeled "Fun," and so many coarse and vulgar absurdities called comical, that it is a welcome relief to see "Comedy—Without Vulgarity" and "A Punch without—brutality."

Young people never had a better picture than this portrayal of their well known "Wizard of Oz." It is perhaps the cleanest and most fascinating of this class of picture, its untiring length is also one of its virtues and successes. A delightfully romantic extravaganza, a spirit of intelligent fun pervades the whole. Never before has so much time and trouble, art and skill been expended on this class of picture, reflecting on L. Frank Baum the greatest credit—a credit to be shared by all his aids. This film must be placed on the Educational list, if for no other reason than to prove the great advance it marks over those of but recent date. It is a higher pioneer for the future.

Although this is not an extended review there are some attractions which should be emphasized. The magic display is unusually good and alluring, bringing about some of the best parts of the photographers' art. The acting of such unusual characters is "thoroughly adequate" and with the radiant beauty of the scenes particularly satisfies. The great majority of young people will want to see it a second or third time, while older people will say to each other: "Forget a while the cares and turmoil of our busy lives, and hie us back to the days of our childhood."

Press comments on "The Patchwork Girl of Oz"

"Altogether the production will prove of value to the exhibitor, because it has the merit of originality and because some parts of the film will send the average audience into roars of laughter.
—*Moving Picture World.*

"The most unique motion picture ever thrown on a screen."
—*San Francisco Call.*

THE IRIS PLEASES A MOTHER

To The Iris:—
Your picture, "Patchwork Girl of Oz," was the finest photoplay I ever saw, and my son and daughter were simply crazy about it; I would not have had them miss it for twenty times 10 cents. To think of the children of Topeka who were not taken to see it makes my heart ache. I want to say that your pictures are worth more to the young than some of the higher branches of schools.

(From Topeka (Kans.) Capital)

"Take care! It is against the Law of Oz to pluck a Six-Leaved Clover."

Above: Screen "title" card from *The Patchwork Girl of Oz* (1914). **Top:** Film still from *His Majesty, the Scarecrow of Oz* (1914), later retitled *The New Wizard of Oz* to capitalize on the success of the first Oz book and stage musical. **Left:** First page of a company advertising brochure (1914).

L. FRANK BAUM
"OZCOT"
AT HOLLYWOOD IN CALIFORNIA

Dec 4, 1916

My dear Carleton H. Lewis

I thank you for your nice letter and the suggestions you offer. Perhaps I can use some of them, but I get so many letters asking me to do contrary things that I can't possibly please all by using their valuable suggestions. However, it proves you're my friend.

Ozily Yours

L Frank Baum

44

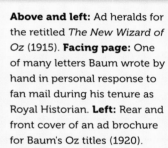

THE OZ FILM COMPANY PRESENTS L. FRANK BAUM'S FAMOUS COMEDY
"THE NEW WIZARD OF OZ"

The New Wizard of Oz

L. FRANK BAUM'S
Famous Comedy

Love, Adventure, Mystifying Sensations, Humorous Surprises and Delicious Comedy in Every Scene !

A WHOLESOME COMEDY THAT WILL PLEASE THE GROWN-UPS AS WELL AS THE CHILDREN.

Featuring the "Scarecrow" and

Above and left: Ad heralds for the retitled *The New Wizard of Oz* (1915). **Facing page:** One of many letters Baum wrote by hand in personal response to fan mail during his tenure as Royal Historian. **Left:** Rear and front cover of an ad brochure for Baum's Oz titles (1920). **Bottom:** Interior of the same flyer, listing the Oz books to date. Reilly & Britton (and the ensuing Reilly & Lee) were the original publishers of all but the first book in the Oz series.

THE TIN WOODMAN of
BY L. FRANK BAUM

Glinda of OZ
by L Frank Baum
Illustrated by Jno R Neill

L. FRANK BAUM
AUTHOR OF
The Famous Oz Books

List of The Oz Books
The Land of Oz.
Ozma of Oz.
Dorothy and the Wizard in Oz.
The Road to Oz.
The Emerald City of Oz.
The Patchwork Girl of Oz.
Tik-Tok of Oz.
The Scarecrow of Oz.
Rinkitink in Oz.
The Lost Princess of Oz.
The Tin Woodman of Oz.
The Magic of Oz.
Glinda of Oz.

For Sale in

GIMBEL BROTHERS'
Land of Oz Toy Store
Fourth Floor

45

An American Phenomenon

The last of L. Frank Baum's Oz titles was published posthumously in 1920; his publishers opened *Glinda of Oz* with the gentle note that "Mr. Baum…went away to take his stories to the little child souls who had lived here too long ago to read the Oz stories for themselves." But an annual Oz book had become both a staple of American youth and the Reilly & Lee catalog, so the search began for a second Royal Historian.

The heir apparent was discovered in Ruth Plumly Thompson, a blithe, endlessly imaginative, self-starting writer who'd made her reputation in contributions to *St. Nicholas* magazine and as the editor of a children's page for the *Philadelphia Public Ledger*. She was 30 when *The Royal Book of Oz* was published in 1921; though only credited with enlarging and editing an unfinished Baum manuscript, the work was entirely hers, and the transition was thus effected.

Below: Whyte & Wyckoff notebooks, utilizing Oz book color plates as their covers (1929). **Facing page:** Ever the aspiring entrepreneur, Frank J. Baum developed a series of Oz dolls in 1924. Unfortunately, the attractive Fabrikoid toys were only minimally marketed; the next year, Reilly & Lee individually boxed and sold his remaining stock of the Scarecrow, the Patchwork Girl, the Tin Woodman, and Jack Pumpkinhead, each with its appropriate Oz book.

As financial mainstay of her widowed mother and invalid sister, Thompson welcomed — and genuinely reveled in — the assignment. Her writing was instantly engaging and vital, much in step with the spirited United States of the 1920s. Throughout the decade, a new Thompson Oz book for the holidays was a happy necessity in thousands of homes, and she was magnificently abetted by the artistry of John R. Neill. His illustrations in the Oz books had become a glorious "given."

Reilly & Lee's advertising forces kept pace with the times as well; their ballyhoo for Oz was more vigorous than ever before. They created wood-cut figures of the Scarecrow and Patchwork Girl as bookstore displays. Their "Scarecrow of Oz Answers Questions by Radio" was a small, magnet-and-cardboard gimmick that posed problems in Oz trivia. From 1926-1928, they revived *The Ozmapolitan*, an "Emerald City newspaper" first invented by Baum in 1904. Each edition offered quixotic gossip about Oz while promoting the latest book and other Reilly & Lee titles.

FRANK BAUM
10807 ROCHESTER AVENUE
LOS ANGELES, 24, CALIFORNIA

THE "SCARECROW" & "TIN WOODMAN" FROM
THE WIZARD OF OZ

SSSSSSSSSSSsssssss   sh!!

Boys · · · · · Girls
Have You Heard About
THE OZMITE CLUB

THE Ozmite Club is a fun Club. *There are no dues.* Membership entitles you to the *Secrets,* the beautiful *Ozmite Club Pin,* copies of the *Ozmapolitan,* the official newspaper of Oz and invitations to the *Oz Parties.*

Who Can Belong??
ANY boy or girl who loves the Oz folk or wants to read about their strange and wonderful adventures recorded in the Oz Books.

How To Join??
Fill in the following blank. Sign your name plainly (at home or down town in the store.)

Check One of these Squares

☐ I am an Ozmite (One who loves the Oz Books. I have read the Oz Books checked (see list on back) and I want to belong to the Ozmite Club.

☐ I have not read any of the Oz Books yet, but I am interested and want to be an Ozmite.

If there are no members of the club in my neighborhood, I will do all I can to get my friends to join so we can get together and enjoy the Ozmite Club and its activities.

My Name Is _____
My Age Is _____
My Next Birthday Is _____
My Address Is _____
My Telephone _____
My Parents Name _____

Where to Join
When you have filled in the blanks properly, hand this sheet to the lady in the book department and she will give you the beautiful Ozmite Pin and Ozmite Secrets.

THE WONDERFUL GAME of OZ

PARKER BROTHERS INC.
SALEM MASS., NEW YORK, LONDON.

Two of the publisher's promotions were particularly effective. In 1926, they established The Ozmite Club "to get groups of children everywhere talking about Oz"; members were invited to apply for a small lapel pin and the "Club Secrets." A year earlier, Thompson herself had helped launch a series of "Oz parties" by writing libretto and lyrics for a Reilly & Lee-promoted *A Day In Oz* playlet. The brief revue — annually revised and utilized over several seasons — was mounted by department stores across the nation. At each venue, local performers were costumed as Oz characters to herald the wonders of the newest book in the series. (Thompson also provided a script for the Jean Gros marionettes and their *The Magical Land of Oz* touring show, beginning in 1928.)

Perhaps not surprisingly, the fans themselves were among the most passionate Oz promoters. The grown-ups who'd fallen in love with the stories 20 years earlier were now in positions of power, and they frequently carried their enthusiasm with them. In 1928, two of Baum's titles were adapted as plays for presentation by the Junior League. (Three more scripts would follow in the 1930s.) Merchandisers began to realize that a licensed tie-in with Oz meant ready consumers. As a result, Parker Brothers issued a stunning board game in 1921, and there were also Oz candies, notebooks, stationery, and party horns.

Among the most ambitious entrepreneurs was Baum's eldest son, Frank Joslyn. Overseas in the military when his father died, Frank envisioned himself as the next Royal Historian. By the time he put himself forth for the job, however, Thompson had already been selected. So the young Baum marketed Oz in his own way, creating a set of character dolls in 1924. The next year, as "L. Frank Baum, Jr.," he cowrote a silent-screen adaptation of *The Wizard of Oz* as a showcase for comic Larry Semon. Unfortunately, the scenario wandered far from the original story: Dorothy was a young flapper and "lost" princess of Oz, which cued in a requisite 1920s romance with "Prince Kynd" of the Emerald City. The Scarecrow, Tin Woodman, Cowardly Lion, and Wizard were only tangentially involved in the manic plot, while "Prime Minister

Below: A cardboard stand-up advertisement for the 1922 Oz book. Kabumpo — "the elegant elephant of Oz" — proved to be one of Ruth Plumly Thompson's most popular creations, and he figured prominently in three of her subsequent stories as well. **Facing page top:** The Ozmite Club's stylish membership lapel pins (1926). **Bottom left:** Oz characters decorated the cover of a Whitman's Wonderbox of children's candy (1926). **Bottom right:** Program cover for the premiere engagement of *The Wizard of Oz* film (1925).

Kruel," "Ambassador Wikked," and "Lady Vishuss" sought to overthrow Dorothy's claim to the throne. The film was a fiasco.

But Oz was so magically entrenched that it survived even such a cinematic mauling. This was quietly demonstrated when the University of Washington Chapbooks published Edward Wagenknecht's *Utopia Americana* (1929). For the first time, an appreciative scholar formally appraised Baum's vision. Although Oz was (and continued to be) all about entertainment, this was its initial recognition as a unique contribution to American literature.

54

M. DeLange présente **ZIGOTO** dans

LE SORCIER D'OZ
LE FILM COMIQUE LE PLUS FANTASTIQUE

Left: A French mini-poster for the 1925 silent film version of *The Wizard of Oz.* Though designed as a showcase for director/star Larry Semon, the motion picture today is notable only for its casting of (a pre-Stan Laurel) Oliver Hardy in the role of a Kansas farmhand who briefly disguises himself as a Tin Woodman. **Below:** Program cover for the film's appearance in Belgium. **Facing page, top left:** Despite its astounding dullness, the Chadwick production was given maximum publicity. This dust jacketed special edition of Baum's book was illustrated with eight movie stills. **Top right:** A glass advertising slide for projection between feature films at theaters due to play Semon's *Wizard.* **Bottom:** A hand-colored lobby card, featuring (from left) Oliver Hardy, G. Howe Black as another Kansas farmhand, Charles Murray as the Wizard, and Semon. (Nepotism note: Dorothy was played by Semon's soon-to-be wife, Dorothy Dwan.)

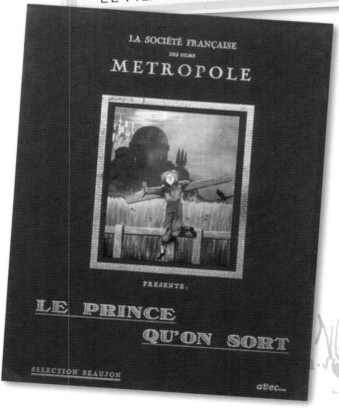

LA SOCIÉTÉ FRANÇAISE DES FILMS
METROPOLE

PRÉSENTE.

LE PRINCE QU'ON SORT

SELECTION BEAUJON   avec...

LARRY SEMON

TROLL-KARLEN FRÅN OZ

Above: A "jointed," hand-colored image of Larry Semon as the Scarecrow. This jumping-jack styled promotional piece was used to advertise the 1925 *Oz*. **Right:** Original preliminary poster art for the film's Swedish release.

Left and below: Reilly & Lee liberally promoted Oz in the 1920s. The Scarecrow and Patchwork Girl figures were designed as in-store heralds for 1926 and 1927 (respectively); a cardboard sign announcing the new Oz book of the year could be slotted in the top of either wooden stand-up. **Bottom center:** This magnetized trivia game was produced in 1924. **Bottom left:** A cutout bookmark advertised the Jean Gros marionette production of *The Magical Land of Oz* (1928).

Right: An early Florence Ryerson/Edgar Allan Woolf *Oz* script; an Adrian apron, tested (but not used) by Judy Garland; and the blouse she wore during the first two weeks of filming. (That footage was scrapped and a new costume fashioned for her.)

A Technicolor Show of Shows

Even as America slid into the Depression, Oz maintained an all-encompassing hold on its public. The Yellow Brick Road provided any traveler the same momentary escape from tribulation as that supplied by the then-prevalent kaleido-scopic film musical numbers of Busby Berkeley. More than just a diversion, however, Oz had become an established tangibility; for millions, it was "real." In casual but salient prose, Ruth Plumly Thompson offered, "A child who may not be able to name offhand the capital of Nebraska or Montana can tell you in a flash the capital of Oz and is often more familiar with its principal rivers, mountains, rulers, points of interest, and historical landmarks than with those of his native state — perhaps because he considers Oz his native state."

While there was some sly and happy self-promotion in her statement, Thompson's "take" was soundly based on the thousands of fan letters she received while deep into a second decade as Royal Historian. Despite the financial vagaries of the times, the Thompson/Neill/Reilly & Lee triumvirate maintained its tradition: there was a new Oz book every year. The series remained the foundation of the phenomenon, and neither author nor illustrator ever flagged in the resourceful addition of eccentrics and escapades to the Ozian landscape.

There was additional Oz promotion as well. In 1932, Reilly & Lee reissued some of Baum's "Little Wizard Stories," capitalizing on a new national craze by repackaging them with jigsaw puzzles of Neill illustrations. A comic serial appeared at the same time, syndicated first to newspapers and then reprinted in comic books. In 1933, enormous statues of the Scarecrow and Tin Woodman were an integral feature of the "Enchanted Island" attraction at the Chicago World's Fair.

The only havoc was caused when Whitman issued *The Laughing Dragon of Oz* (1935), a "Big Little Book" written by Baum's son, Frank Joslyn. Reilly & Lee brought suit; their contract with Baum's widow gave them publishing rights to any Oz sequels. Whitman quickly

Above: 1939 insert poster for MGM's *The Wizard of Oz*.

agreed to let the book drift out of print and abandoned plans for a second title, *The Enchanted Princess of Oz.*

Meanwhile, authorized dramatizations continued to emerge. The Meglin Kiddies, a troupe of Los Angeles-area performing children, appeared in a two-reel *The Land of Oz* film in 1932. The next year, Ted Eshbaugh produced a brief, animated *The Wizard of Oz*, historically notable for the fact that the opening Kansas sequence was tinted only in shades of black-and-white and blue; when Dorothy and Toto fell out of a cyclonic sky into Oz, they and their surroundings suddenly evolved into Technicolor. The most far-reaching (if short-lived) Ozian reenactment was delivered directly into millions of homes when the National Broadcasting Company brought adaptations of the first six Oz books to radio. There were three, "live" fifteen-minute shows per week from September 25, 1933, through March 23, 1934, and each opened with the portentous words of announcer Ben Grauer: "Jell-O presents *The Wizard of Oz!*"

Below: "The Wonderland of Oz" map, distributed as a premium in conjunction with the 1932-33 newspaper cartoon serialization of 443 Oz "strips."

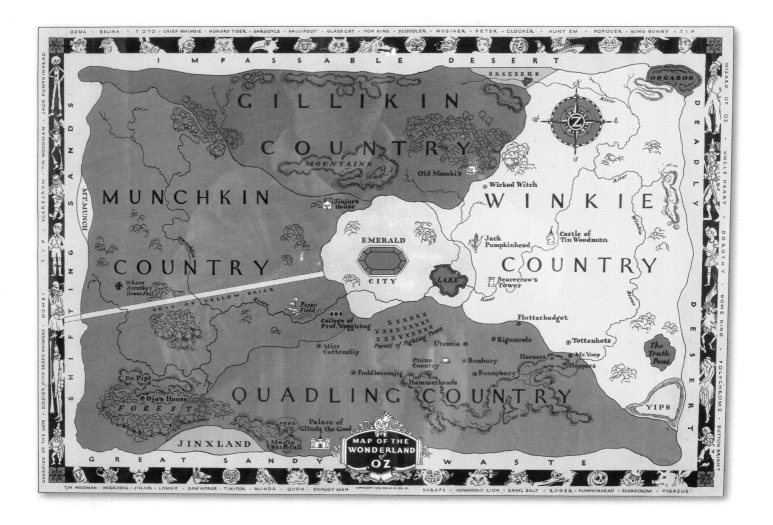

60

Above left: Some of "The Wonderland of Oz" serials were later adapted and reprinted as comic book features. **Top:** The cover of the giveaway scrapbook, provided to children who wanted to clip, mount, and save the strips. **Above:** This circular was sent to newspaper editors to solicit syndication contracts for the series. **Left:** In 1933-34, Jell-O promotional pages were added to four of Baum's "Little Wizard Stories" booklets and given as premiums in conjunction with the NBC Oz radio series.

But every preceding (and, as it turned out, subsequent) Oz dramatic adaptation would fade into comparative obscurity with the 1939 release of MGM's Technicolor motion picture. There had been years of conjecture about a possible Oz feature — for Eddie Cantor as the Scarecrow, for W.C. Fields as the Wizard, for Mary Pickford, Helen Hayes, Shirley Temple, or Marcia Mae Jones as Dorothy. But only MGM could risk $3.2 million and manifest the resources (on either side of the camera) for a live-action fantasy. Their *The Wizard of Oz* was envisioned both as a showcase for fast-rising 16-year-old contract player Judy Garland and as an "integrated" musical, in which songs and dances were an inherent part of the storytelling process.

Fraught with script, concept, casting, and production delays, the Victor Fleming/Mervyn LeRoy/Arthur Freed film took — from

Left and below: Reilly & Lee boxed four of Baum's "Little Wizard Stories" with jigsaw puzzles in 1932. **Facing page:** The back cover of a Jell-O Oz booklet.

63

Below right: The Scarecrow can be seen as one of the engraved characters on this collectible key from the 1933 World's Fair "Enchanted Island." The key rests on the cover of *A Beautiful Model of the Enchanted Island,* a do-it-yourself kit and souvenir of the exposition. **Below:** A cutout representation of the Island's Tin Woodman statue from the same book. **Facing page:** To tie-in with a contemporary publishing fad, Bobbs-Merrill licensed a 1934 Waddle Book edition of *The Wizard of Oz,* which included bound-in cardboard cutouts of Oz characters. Once detached and assembled, they could "walk" down an accompanying "Yellow Brick" ramp.

proposal to premiere — nearly two years to realize. Plans for its promotion induced MGM to establish a corporate merchandising force; they realized only limited success in their initial efforts but nevertheless licensed more than a score of Oz products.

The finished film itself knew few limitations; it broke attendance records across the nation and won mostly euphoric reviews. (One or two of the few dissenting critics were subsequently publicly taken to task by their fellow journalists.) And even though its status as a legend and icon was decades in the future, nothing apart from Baum's original book would have more ultimate importance and resonance in the first 100 years of Oz than MGM's *Wizard.*

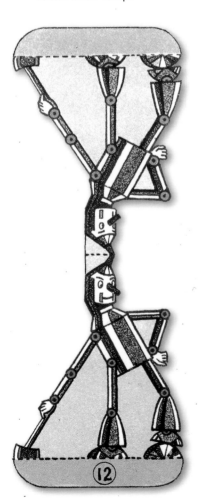

Below: A bag of "magic sand from along the yellow brick road," given away in theater lobbies to promote the forthcoming appearance of MGM's *The Wizard of Oz* (1939). **Below right:** A 1939 Hollywood trade paper ad (August 14, 1939), heralding the next evening's premiere of the picture.

MAGIC SAND

from along the yellow brick road to the land of Oz! Place it under your pillow— your dreams will come true when you see . . .

THE WIZARD OF

O z

with
Judy GARLAND
Frank MORGAN
Ray BOLGER
Bert LAHR
Jack HALEY

PHOTOGRAPHED IN TECHNICOLOR

COLONIAL THEATRE

METRO · GOLDWYN · MAYER'S TECHNICOLOR MARVEL

"The WIZARD of OZ"

IS ONE OF THE GREAT PICTURES OF ALL TIME, PERHAPS THE GREATEST PICTURE EVER MADE! BEYOND YOUR WILDEST DREAMS ARE ITS TECHNICOLOR WONDERS, AS THOUSANDS OF LIVING ACTORS CREATE SCREEN MAGIC TO THRILL THE WORLD!

Preview—
PREMIERE
TOMORROW NIGHT at 8:30
TUESDAY, AUGUST 15
GRAUMAN'S CHINESE

SEATS *Now*
THEATRE BOX OFFICE
ALL AGENCIES...Or CALL ASHLEY 43311
EXTENSION 396   ALL SEATS $2.20

M·G·M'S Wonder Show "THE WIZARD OF OZ" with Judy Garland · Frank Morgan · Ray Bolger · Bert Lahr · Jack Haley Billie Burke · Margaret Hamilton Charley Grapewin and The Munchkins · A VICTOR FLEMING Production · Screen Play by Noel Langley, Florence Ryerson and Edgar Allan Woolf · From the Book by L. Frank Baum Directed by Victor Fleming Produced by MERVYN LeROY
3263

REGULAR ENGAGEMENT at LOEW'S STATE and GRAUMAN'S CHINESE Starts WEDNESDAY

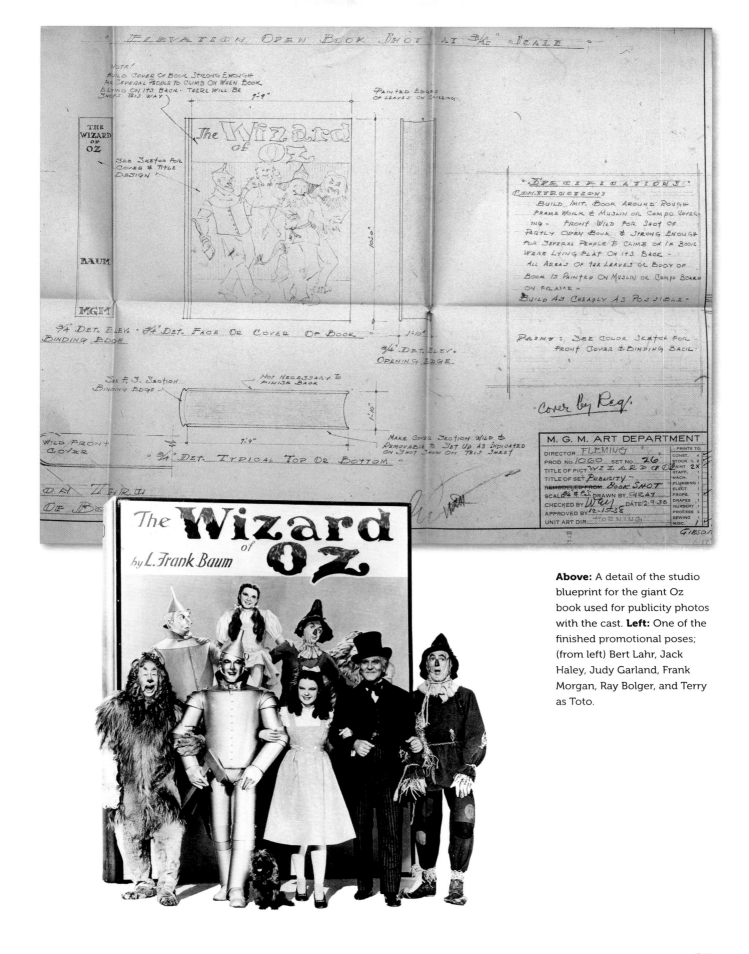

Above: A detail of the studio blueprint for the giant Oz book used for publicity photos with the cast. **Left:** One of the finished promotional poses; (from left) Bert Lahr, Jack Haley, Judy Garland, Frank Morgan, Ray Bolger, and Terry as Toto.

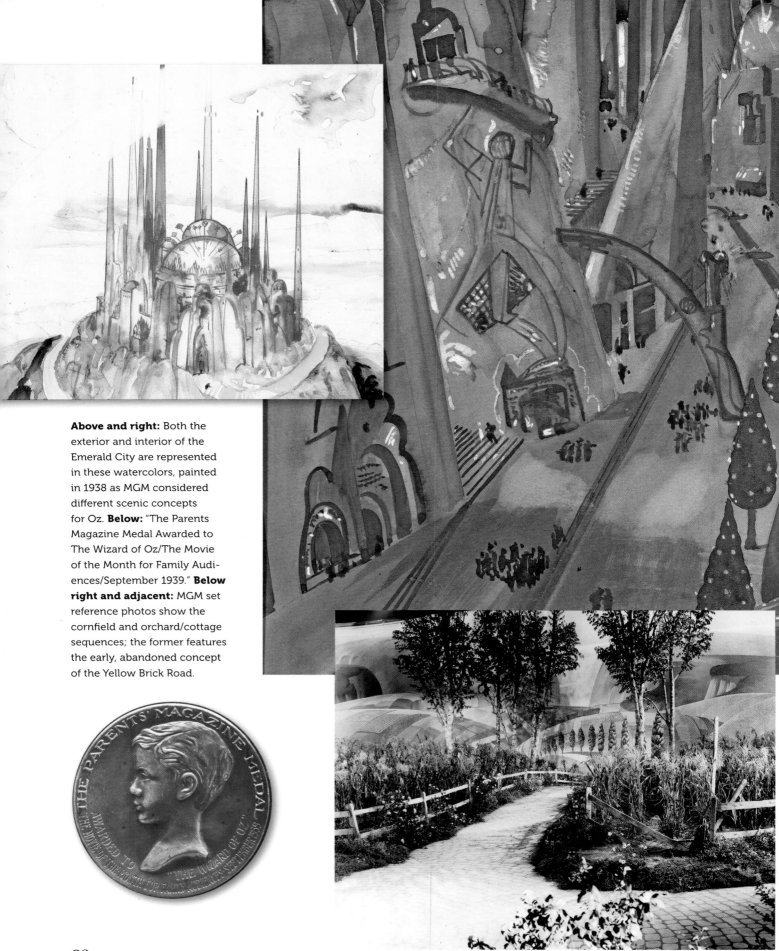

Above and right: Both the exterior and interior of the Emerald City are represented in these watercolors, painted in 1938 as MGM considered different scenic concepts for Oz. **Below:** "The Parents Magazine Medal Awarded to The Wizard of Oz/The Movie of the Month for Family Audiences/September 1939." **Below right and adjacent:** MGM set reference photos show the cornfield and orchard/cottage sequences; the former features the early, abandoned concept of the Yellow Brick Road.

Top: Lyric sheet distributed at rehearsal to the (approximately) 124 "Munchkins" of *Oz* so that they could memorize their musical sequence, plus the work agreement signed by "Munchkin Mayor" Charles Becker. **Above:** Publicity manual for the MGM film, including production history, cast biographies, and prewritten promotional features for use by print media.

Right: As the epitome of villainy, Margaret Hamilton threatened the life of Judy Garland with this hourglass. For more than four decades, MGM's *Oz* props and costumes have set record prices at auctions and sales.

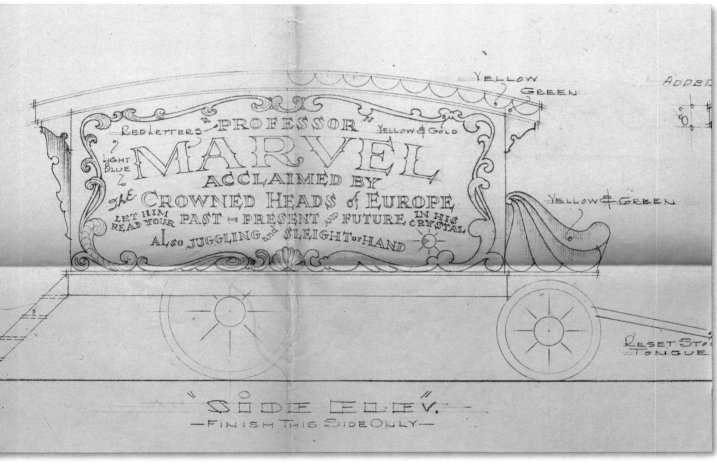

Top: Photo triptych of a special guest star of the 1939 Macy's Thanksgiving Day Parade in New York City.
Above: Detail of the studio blueprint for Professor Marvel's Wagon.

Facing page: The original, handmade heavy-felt costume worn by Jerry Maren, central member of MGM's "Lollipop Guild" trio. **Above:** Autographed Maren photo, showing his presentation of a Munchkinland souvenir to Judy Garland. **Right:** Drawings of scenes from the *Oz* film decorate this 1939 Brian Fabrics scarf. **Far right:** Australian ad flyer for the movie's appearance "Down Under" (1940).

72

Above: MGM created one of these "door hanger" advertising pieces for each member of the principal cast. Note the misspelling of Billie Burke's first name. **Right:** The box cover and one of the "Hangers from The Merrie Land of Oz," manufactured by Barney Stempler & Sons.

Far Left: Corning Glass-works manufactured several Oz glasses as premiums for Sealtest Cottage Cheese, but this Garland prototype was never commercially marketed. It may have been envisioned as part of a second series.
Left: One of a dozen Oz Valentines issued in 1940 and 1941 by the American Colortype Company. **Bottom:** The Dart Board Equipment Company box cover and game board for their 1939 tie-in to the MGM film. The product was never mass-manufactured, and only a few test samples are known to exist. Even the readily-available Oz merchandise licensed by MGM enjoyed but a limited shelf life, as it was so specifically aligned to theatrical bookings for the film (which ran from August 1939 until early 1940).

Above: Hollow, molded-rubber Cowardly Lion squeeze toy from the A. A. Burnstein Sales Organization (1939). **Above left:** The Kerk Guild manufactured this boxed set of "Five Soapy Characters from the Land of Oz" as an MGM tie-in in 1939. **Left:** Diverse dramatizations of Oz stories had begun to flourish in the 1920s and permeated the 1930s, thus helping to pave the way for the Garland movie musical. These Dorothy and Toto hand puppets were designed in connection with a WPA Museum project in 1932. **Facing page:** In 1939, the Ideal Novelty & Toy Company issued 13", 15.5", and 18" "Judy Garland as Dorothy" dolls, and 17" and 21" "The Strawman by Ray Bolger" dolls. Shown here are the mid-size Judy, with the larger Bolger positioned above her. Meanwhile, each of the four smaller Scarecrows boasts variant clothing.

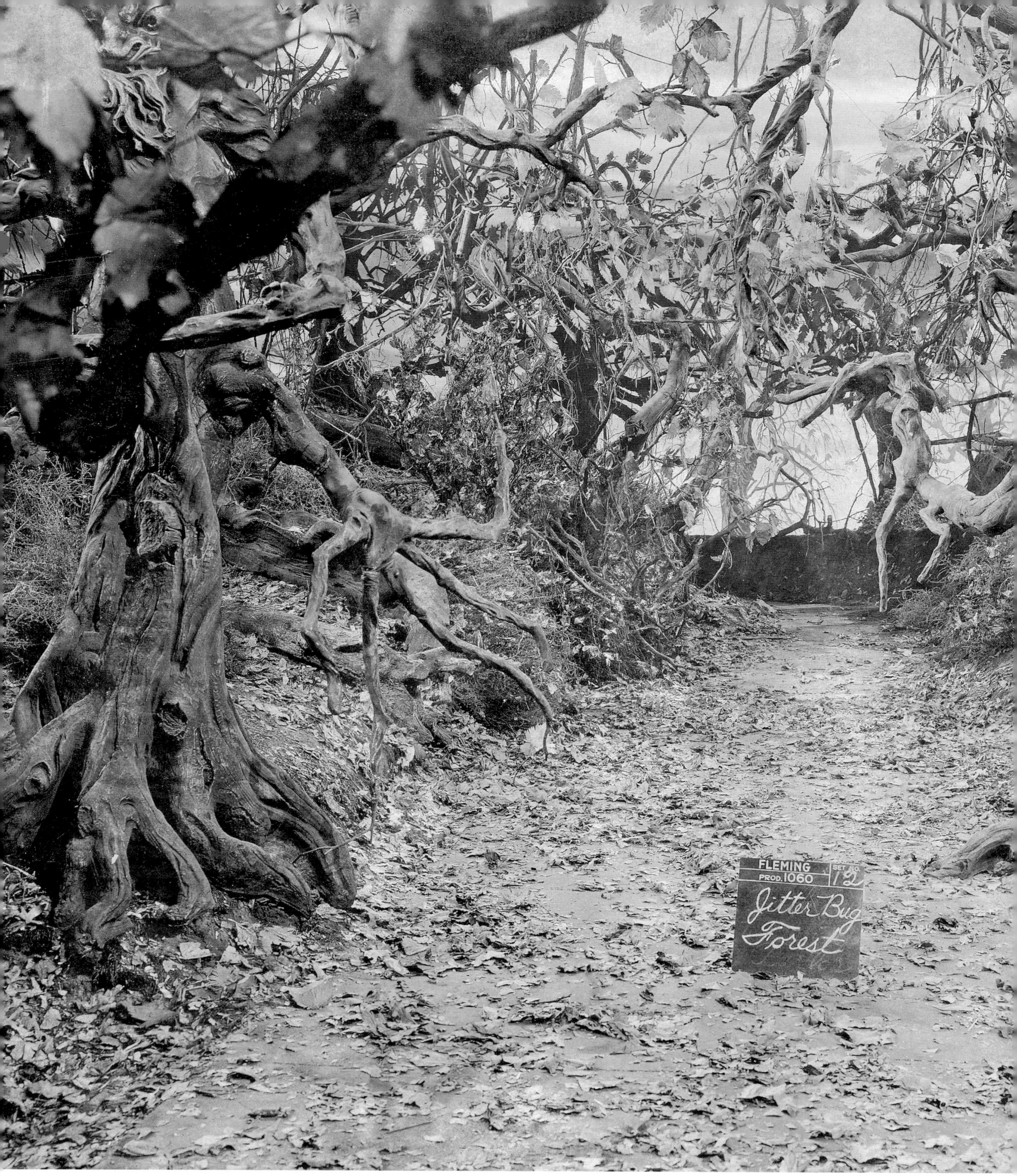
FLEMING
PROD. 1060
SET NO 12
Jitter Bug
Forest

Above: Only around a dozen actors were actually costumed and "flown" as Winged Monkeys in MGM's *Oz*. Scores more were created as eight-inch rubber miniatures and manipulated by wires from the sound stage rafters; very few of these survive. **Left:** Set reference still for the attack-of-the-monkeys sequence — and the deleted song-and-dance, "The Jitterbug."

Oz Around the World

The *Wizard of Oz* was one of the top-grossing films of 1939 and an Academy Award nominee as Best Picture. In the annual *Film Daily* poll of more than 450 critics, it ranked among the ten best movies of the year. But due to an odd combination of factors, MGM's musical lost about $750,000 in its initial release. Though theaters enjoyed turn-away business, around two-thirds of the *Oz* audience was comprised of children, who paid substantially less admission than did adults. The glut of incoming, pre-booked film product often meant that *Oz* couldn't be held over in many cities, even though attendance warranted extended engagements. Most detrimental to its income, however, was the loss of much of the potential foreign market; World War II began in Europe in September 1939, two weeks after the American *Oz* premiere.

Above: MGM's *The Wizard of Oz* in Italy (1947). **Left:** Cover art for an illustrated cinema program from Austria (1940). **Far left:** Swedish poster art (1940). **Facing page:** Spanish poster art (1945).

While some foreign countries were able to exhibit *Oz* in 1940, many others had to wait until after the war was over in 1945. But whenever it was finally seen, the film provided literary inspiration around the world: the 1940s marked the first regular appearance of Oz books in foreign languages. A few of them were based on (or at least illustrated by) material from the film. The vast majority were straight-forward translations or adaptations of the original Baum story. No matter the source, however, the books proved (and remain) fascinating primarily because of their artwork. The characters and countrysides of Oz continually provoked a spectrum of wildly diverse illustrative concepts.

The 1940s also brought changes and disruptions in the American Oz book series for the first time in two decades. Ruth Plumly Thompson wrote her 19th volume in 1939; *Ozoplaning with the Wizard of Oz* was titled to tie in with the MGM film. She then "resigned," momentarily drained by her long-term commitment to the series and its fans. For the sake of continuity, Reilly & Lee approached John R. Neill to both author and illustrate the Oz book for 1940. His writing — though flamboyant and inventive — was only partially as successful as his draftsmanship, but he contributed three titles in all before his death in 1943. At that point, the publishers put the series on hiatus

Above and top: The cover and representative artwork from the 1962 Latvian edition of *The Wizard of Oz* serve as prime examples of the surge of foreign *Oz* books that began in the 1940s and never abated. **Left:** A French film magazine for 1940, promoting the forthcoming *Oz* film.

until after the war; in 1946 and 1949, they issued manuscripts written by Jack Snow, a lifelong Baum aficionado and scholar. Though well-crafted, Snow's stories lacked humor; the illustrations by Frank Kramer were affable, though missing the beauty and finer touches of Neill's work. Both books sold less well than had the earlier titles, and Reilly & Lee felt the series might well have run its course.

Oz nonetheless remained in the nation's consciousness. There were a few new product licensings (most notably an association with Swift's peanut butter "spread") and, even though the MGM film disappeared from theaters after second and third-run engagements in 1940, its songs continued to grow in popularity. MGM first made the *Oz* musical score and orchestrations available to the St. Louis Muny Opera for a summer theater production of *The Wizard* in 1942. Other professional theaters around the world soon clamored for the chance to present *Oz* on stage. Although the script of those early versions was adapted from Baum's book rather than from the film screenplay, the songs throughout were primarily those written for the movie by Harold Arlen and E.Y. Harburg. Their music and lyrics had first enjoyed special attention in 1939 when Decca released a set of 78-rpm *Oz* records featuring Judy Garland and the Ken Darby Singers. This was available throughout the 1940s, as were other renditions of

Top: This theater program accompanied the first appearance of MGM's *Oz* in Japan (1955) and provided a synopsis of the plot along with stills and artwork. **Above:** *American Movie Weekly* — a Japanese program magazine (1955). **Right:** Ad flyer for the film's initial appearance in Yugoslavia (circa 1940s).

Above: The box cover and illustrated contents of "The Wizard of Oz Card Game" from London's Castell Brothers Ltd. (1940).

the *Oz* score. In 1949, Capitol issued a record album based on Baum's fourth title, *Dorothy and the Wizard in Oz;* it was a clever marketing move, as MGM that year reissued *The Wizard of Oz.*

The re-release was a triumph for the studio, proof positive that a market existed for classic older films. *Oz* once again garnered superlative reviews and took in enough at the box office to put the picture firmly in the black. Its reappearance was also a cheerful reminder of general Oz omnipresence, even if public sensibility about the series had settled comfortably into second-nature.

As it turned out, both the film and the book on which it was based were on the brink of a genuinely colossal resurgence. The second half of the twentieth century would see *Oz* explode into public consciousness as had no other American fairy tale or motion picture — and ultimately command a plateau of singular, unparalleled prominence.

METRO-GOLDWYN-MAYERS STORA FÄRGFILM ÄR BYGGD PÅ DENNA BOK

TROLLKARLEN

från OZ AV L. FRANK BAUM

BILDER AV W. W. DENSLOW I FÄRG OCH I SVART OCH VITT

Il mago di OZ

NEL RACCONTO DI
MARIA ROSARIA
BERARDI, TRATTO
DAL FILM OMONIMO

Above: With the gradual widespread international exhibition of MGM's *Oz*, several foreign editions of the book capitalized on the film characters. *Trollkarlen fran Oz* appeared in Sweden in 1940. **Right:** *Il Mago di Oz* was published in Italy in 1947.

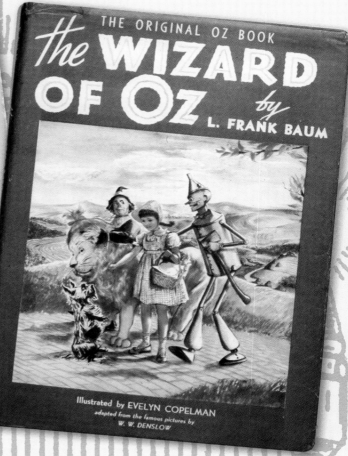

Above left: *O Feiticeiro de Oz* was marketed in 1946 in Portugal. **Above:** In 1944, the original Denslow artwork was dropped from American editions of *The Wizard of Oz,* and publisher Bobbs-Merrill had new pictures drawn by Evelyn Copelman. Her concepts, vastly different than Denslow's, also were inspired by the MGM film. Countless copies of the Copelman-illustrated *Wizard* have since been printed; her work remains among the most familiar and treasured of any Oz artist. **Left:** Ozzy stationery utilized by two "Royal Historians" in their voluminous fan correspondence.

Right: The reverse of the Yugoslav flyer shown on page 84. **Far right:** Prerelease publicity: *Oz* on a magazine cover in Uruguay, November 17, 1939. **Below:** Promotion flyer for the film's debut in Brazil (1940).

Left: The only known copy of the glorious two-panel billboard for the MGM film, designed in France by pre-eminent contemporary poster artist, "Grinsson." **Above:** MGM's official photo-and-Hirschfeld *Oz* stationery, distributed by the studio for in-house and promotional use in (at least) English and Spanish.

89

Above: The Capitol Records adaptation of Baum's fourth Oz book was conceived (and illustrated) to cash in on the 1949 United States reissue of the MGM film. **Right:** The cover of MGM's 1949 recording, in which an orchestra and chorus re-created the movie songs. **Above right**: The theater program for the film's initial release in Yugoslavia (circa 1940s).

Left: *The Wizard of Oz* is abridged for readers in Argentina (1947). **Below:** The *Oz* "Model-Craft" kit was available during the 1940s and 1950s, enabling children to mold and paint their own Oz figurines.

oodman's sundae

OZ Peanut Butter Fudge
...ead heart cut

Wonderful
recipes with
Swift's **OZ** peanut butter

MARTHA LOGAN   HOME ECONOMIST   SWIFT & COMPANY

the WIZARD of OZ BOOK STORY

OZ COMES HOME

After their first exposure to *The Wizard of Oz* via the 1949 MGM reissue, millions of children manifested the same ardor as had their parents — and grandparents. Consequently, 1950-1952 saw a proliferation of publications for youngsters: a picture-book abridgement, Oz additions to the Little Golden and Wonder Books series, and even a new title from Reilly & Lee. In 1951, they issued Rachel Cosgrove's *The Hidden Valley of Oz* which, in best Baum tradition, sent an American child soaring through the air (this time via runaway kite) to an eventual denouement in the Emerald City. Jack Snow returned to the post of Royal Historian three years later and assembled profiles of more than 600 Oz characters for *Who's Who in Oz*. Though a sales disappointment (faithful readers sought a story, not an encyclopedia), the book was indication of both the scope and believability of all that had been wrought by Baum and Company since 1900.

In 1956, Oz won further respect when the Columbia University Libraries paid homage to Baum's centennial in a resplendent exhibition of his work. That same year, the copyright expired on *The Wizard of Oz*, which meant an astronomical new level of visibility for the first Oz book. Though sales figures for past printings already topped four million copies, its public domain status meant that anyone could produce a new edition of the story or utilize its characters; a parade of products began immediately.

It was a propitious time for such excitement; those who cared about Oz were about to be aggressively challenged. For decades, there had been a pointed antipathy to fantasy from scattered librarians, educators, and historians. (Their limited perspective was dryly

Above: Insert poster for the 1955 reissue of MGM's *Oz*.
Left and facing page: By the 1950s, one of the most visible commercial tie-ins with Baum's first story and characters was manifested by Swift's Oz peanut butter, heralded via promotional pens, coloring books, and recipe suggestions.

summarized by author Martin Gardner: "How could anything so popular, they say to themselves, be anything but trash? Of course it never occurs to them to *read* an Oz book and decide for themselves.") The negative faction sank to its all-time low in 1957. Echoing the disdain of compatriots in Florida and Washington, D.C., the director of the Detroit library system publicly announced there was "nothing uplifting or elevating" about Baum's work; he accused the Oz books of "negativism" and a "cowardly approach to life." Oz books were summarily banned from the shelves of some libraries — if they had carried them at all.

Clockwise from below :
Japanese edition of *The Wizard of Oz* (1955), Japanese mini-poster for the MGM film (1955; using artwork from the U.S. "Wonder Book" abridgment), Japanese MGM herald (1955), Turkish edition of *The Wizard of Oz* (circa 1950s), and another Japanese/MGM promotional flyer (1955). **Bottom:** Endpapers by Anton Loeb for the 1950 Random House *Oz* picture book. In print for more than two decades, this edition provided an initial introduction to Baum's story for countless youngsters.

In response, there was for the first time a figurative rush to the Ozzy barricades by prestigious journalists, teachers, and more knowledgeable librarians; the public outcry was enough to effect (if gradually) the reinstatement — and even further recognition — of all things Oz. As Gardner later reported, "Oz fans [began] to cry out against this conspiracy…and to say, without being in the least ashamed, that the Royal History is a great and enduring work of American Literature." He and Russell Nye coauthored a 1957 appreciation of Baum, *The Wizard of Oz and Who He Was;* it was just the first of many successful volleys from esteemed writers that either educated or muzzled any non-fans.

Perhaps the fervor of 1957 was impelled by what in retrospect would be the most significant event of the preceding year: the television premiere of the MGM film. A second theatrical reissue in 1955 had been unevenly promoted, but its limited success meant nothing when the TV ratings were posted for November 3, 1956; more than 45 million people had been

Above: MGM issued its first *Oz* soundtrack record in conjunction with the film's television debut in 1956. A perennial best-seller, the disc innovatively combined songs and dialogue lifted directly from the film print. **Left:** The first incarnations of Swift's product had appeared in the 1940s — as "peanut spread."

spellbound for two hours. Few families could then boast a color set, and most viewers saw the picture in black and white. But even under those conditions, the film had found a new home.

The TV host that evening was the Cowardly Lion himself, Bert Lahr, and he was joined in emcee duties by the "daughter of Dorothy," ten-year-old Liza Minnelli. ("Mama" Judy watched on a backstage TV at Broadway's Palace Theater where she was starring in her own show.) A more significant on-camera presence, however, was that of an Oz collector from Brooklyn, whom the producers remembered from publicity he'd received as a contributor to the Columbia exhibition. They invited him — and his first edition of *The Wizard* — to appear with Lahr and Minnelli; Justin Schiller was just 13 years old.

Two months later, that same indefatigable teen channeled his enthusiasm into the formation of The International Wizard of Oz Club, with 16 charter members (most much older than he) and a four-page mimeographed "newspaper" ingenuously titled *The Baum Bugle*. It was quiet indication of Ozmania-to-come; by the 1980s, the club had become the preeminent Oz fan base, and the *Bugle* was a professionally designed magazine with thousands of annual subscribers. 🐾

Below: *Bibliographia Oziana* and two issues of *The Baum Bugle* — among many publications of The International Wizard of Oz Club since 1957.
Facing page: Fabric detail from a woman's dress; catalog for the 1956 Baum centenary exhibition; and original art by Dick Martin for the title page of *The Musical Fantasies of L. Frank Baum* (1958; inscribed to his coauthor Alla T. Ford). Newspaper ad art for the third national telecast of MGM's *Oz* (December 11, 1960). CBS initially used its own network stars and their children to emcee the program; shown at top left are Richard Boone (*Have Gun, Will Travel*) and son Peter.

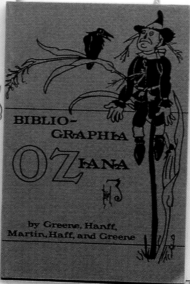

OFF to SEE the WIZARD

For all of its preceding fame, Oz now reached a new zenith of celebrity. The larger percentage of that renown was due to the MGM film; it enjoyed an unprecedented 10 national telecasts between 1960-1970 and never placed lower than fourth in any weekly ratings poll. By mid-decade, children had come to anticipate the annual TV appearance of *The Wizard of Oz* as a family event on a par with their birthdays and the December holidays.

Appropriately, the picture's popularity kindled an overall passion for the subject that revitalized every aspect of Oz. By happy coincidence, Henry Regnery had purchased Reilly & Lee in 1959; under his guidance, the company embarked on a vigorous marketing and promotional policy. Among other activities, they issued a full-length biography of Baum, adapted his 1904-1905 comic strip into a deluxe *The Visitors From Oz* volume, brought out picture books of four of his *Oz* stories, and added a 40th title — *Merry Go Round in Oz* (1963) — to the official series. The latter was written by the distinguished children's author Eloise Jarvis McGraw (with considerable input from her daughter, Lauren Lynn); it was illustrated by lifelong Baum devotee, Dick Martin, whose bright drawings or designs had become an irrevocable part of literally every Regnery/Oz project.

The general furor also brought about fresh examination of Baum's life work in publications as diverse as *American Heritage, The Reader's Digest*, and *The American Book Collector*. Majority opinion throughout was not only sympathetic but often downright laudatory in the long-delinquent acknowledgment that America had possessed in Frank Baum its own Hans Christian Andersen or Brothers Grimm.

Equally enthusiastic was the media attention paid to an ever-more-active International Wizard of Oz Club. When their annual "Oz Convention" was described in a casual *Saturday Review* column in 1963, the notice brought in scores of new members, as did much of the ensuing journalistic scrutiny of their endeavors. Such

Above: A Mattel jack-in-the-box was one of many products licensed in conjunction with the *Off to See the Wizard* TV series (1967). **Facing page:** Baum's "flying machine" Gump was recreated as an assembled paper cutout by Dick Martin to promote *The Visitors From Oz* (1960); the next year, he illustrated four Oz picture books.

consideration was warranted, for the Club quite often stood at the forefront of any developing Oz enterprise. As their roster grew, they were able to augment *The Baum Bugle* with a publishing program of Oz maps, out-of-print books and rare Baum material, and a definitive bibliography of the complex printing history of the Oz series.

By now, several of those early Oz books were in the public domain. Separately or coupled with the much-loved MGM movie songs, Baum's stories and characters thus figured prominently in dramatic presentations throughout the 1960s. Their venues ranged from ice shows and the circus to puppet plays and television programs. Shirley Temple played both Princess Ozma and her alter ego (an enchanted lad named Tip) in an hour-long NBC teleplay of *The Land of Oz* in 1960.

A year later, Alfred Rankin and Jules Bass debuted 130 five-minute *Tales of the Wizard of Oz* cartoons, which ran in syndication throughout North America. They further parlayed their Oz connection into a much-publicized (albeit poorly received) NBC animated special, *Return to Oz*, in 1964. As early as 1961, there had been preliminary negotiations for an MGM cartoon series in which Judy Garland

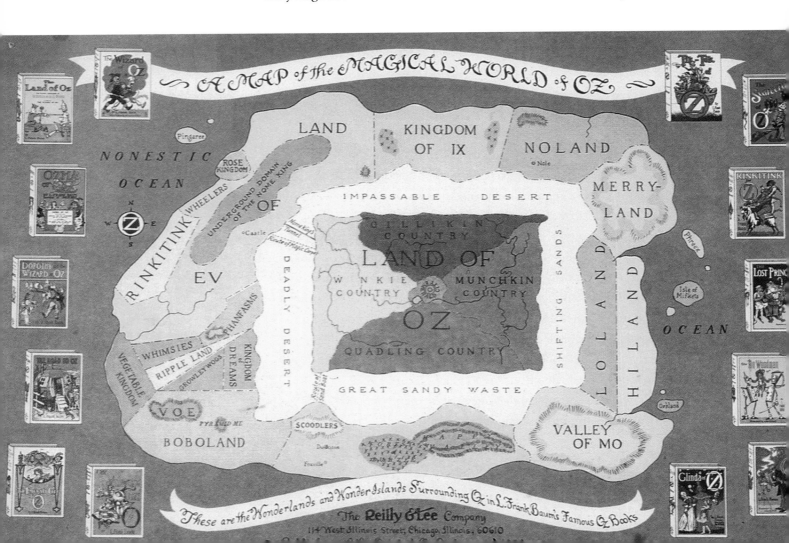

Above: Oz books with new Dick Martin dust jackets (1960) are flanked by Progressive Art Products bookends (1971). **Left:** *The Wizard of Oz* as read in Russia (1961) and Israel (1963). **Facing page top:** Curad bandages were an *Off to See the Wizard* tie-in (1967). **Bottom:** A Reilly & Lee Oz map, designed by Dick Martin to promote new hardcover editions of the 14 Baum titles issued in 1964-1965.

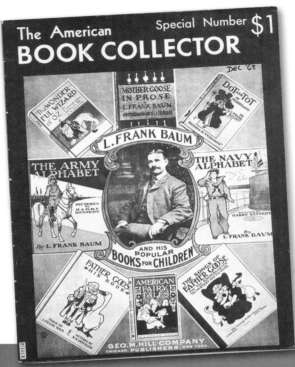

would vocally re-create the role of Dorothy Gale. Instead, the studio later produced *Off To See the Wizard*, which utilized their own animated Oz characters as hosts of weekly family film fare over ABC-TV in 1967-1968.

Such nonstop multimedia activity also resulted in the most massive amount of Oz merchandising to that time. Though many products were related to the various TV shows, even random Oz ware began to hit the marketplace with increasing popularity. In 1969, exploitation emerged on its grandest scale with the launching of a "Land of Oz" theme park near Banner Elk, North Carolina. Though much off the regular tourist beat and comparatively inaccessible near the summit of Beech Mountain, the park still managed to draw enthralled children and their families who thrilled to an adventure tour much inspired by the MGM film.

Above: Books about Baum and Oz began with *Utopia Americana* (1929), continued with *The Wizard of Oz and Who He Was* (1957) and *The Musical Fantasies of L. Frank Baum* (1958), and peaked with *To Please a Child* (1961), the latter coauthored by journalist Russell P. MacFall. The majestic *The Annotated Wizard of Oz* (1973) and a children's treatment, *L. Frank Baum* (1995), were among many subsequent accounts. **Left:** Dick Martin's dazzling Oz book poster (1965). **Facing page top:** *The American Book Collector* devoted an entire issue to Baum in 1962. **Bottom:** *Merry Go Round in Oz* (1963), the new "white" editions of the Baum Oz books (1964-65), and their respective promotional leaflets.

Above: Oz recordings have proliferated across the decades, beginning in the 1950s when Baum's original story became public domain. Some featured MGM songs or original music; one conveyed the entire text of the first Oz book.

Perhaps the most telling measure of the force of Oz in the 1960s is that its happily emotional resonance continued to grow and affect all ages — despite increasing societal turmoil and world unrest. The premature death of Judy Garland in June 1969 provided a poignant underscoring to the innocence and importance of Baum's story; a world "where there isn't any trouble…somewhere over the rainbow" was perhaps more to be desired, more a necessary haven to be treasured than ever before.

Left and above: Prospectus and ad art for Shirley Temple's 1960-1961 TV series, which kicked off with an adaptation of the second Oz book. The cast included Agnes Moorehead, Jonathan Winters, Sterling Holloway, Arthur Treacher, Ben Blue, Gil Lamb, Frances Bergen, and Mel Blanc.

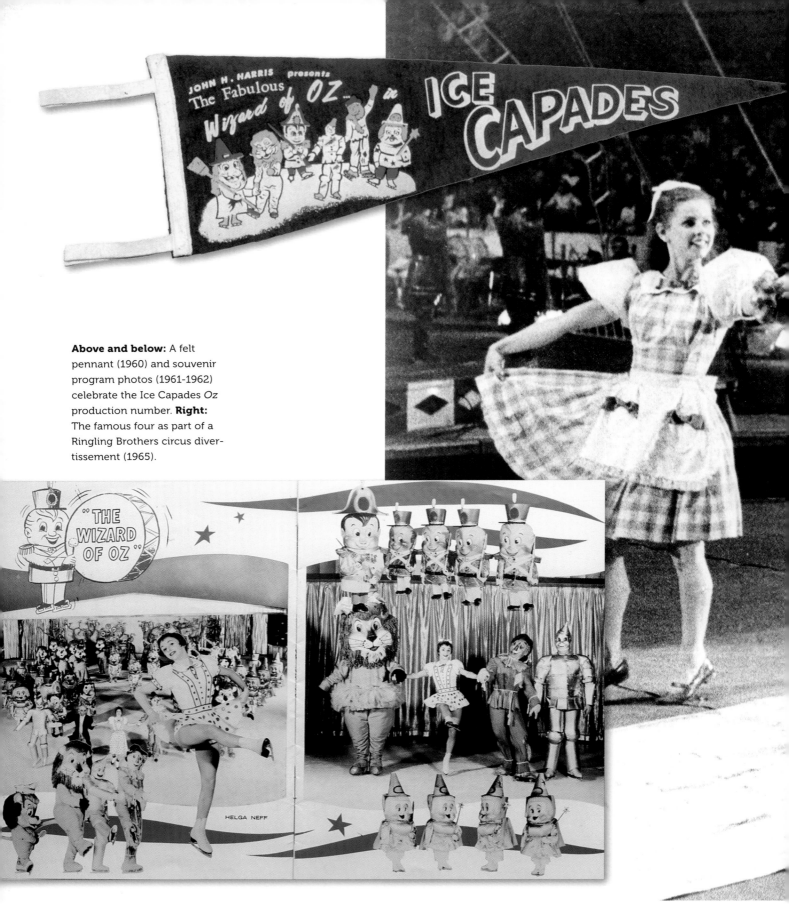

Above and below: A felt pennant (1960) and souvenir program photos (1961-1962) celebrate the Ice Capades *Oz* production number. **Right:** The famous four as part of a Ringling Brothers circus divertissement (1965).

HELGA NEFF

108

Above: An animation cel and matching background from the Rankin & Bass NBC-TV special, *Return to Oz* (1964). **Right:** Loew Company's "Wizard Slate from Oz" reflected and promoted the production company's earlier, less-ambitiously drawn *Tales of the Wizard of Oz* cartoon series (1961).

Left and Above: Other 1961-1963 Rankin & Bass commercial tie-ins included a Ponytail coin purse, Whitman coloring book, and Dorothy and "Dandy Lion" dolls from the Artistic Toy Company.

Below: The Rankin & Bass *Return to Oz* appeared briefly on videotape in 1986. The original 1964 telecast had been widely advertised by General Electric, which also offered a charm bracelet of the show's characters as a premium. **Right:** A full-production *Oz* ice show was first mounted in the United Kingdom in 1962, foreshadowing by three decades a similar United States skating extravaganza.

Left and below: Program cover for the Oz marionette adaptation performed off-Broadway by the renowned Bill Baird (1968). A contemporary Dorothy marionette drew its design from the Garland/MGM approach to the role. **Bottom:** Australia's "live," Oz-on-stage was advertised by a small banner that could also be worn as a wrap-around hat.

Bil Baird Theater
59 barrow st. new york 10014

MONs. to THUs. 10.15 & 2
"The Wizard of Oz"
TiVOLi ON STAGE
FIRST TIME — IN AUSTRALIA!
FRIs. & SATs. 2 & 8 pm.
ON STAGE TiVOLi

Wizard of Oz Flicker Ring
With Display $11.25
Without Display $11.00

per bag of 1M

©67 samsons products

OFF TO SEE THE WIZARD ©67 MGM

1¢

Below: The Rankin & Bass cartoons inspired Halco Halloween masks (early 1960s). **Left:** A "flicker ring" collection (here on its display card) offered character concepts from ABC-TV's *Off to See the Wizard* (1967); the rings then were accessed via gumball machines. **Bottom:** The Banner Elk (North Carolina) "Land of Oz" theme park created its own approach to Baum's denizens (1969-1980). **Facing page top:** Oversized metal ornaments for use in public parks in the 1960s: the Tin Woodman topped garbage cans and the Scarecrow served as a mid-board seesaw decoration. **Bottom:** Louis Marx & Company wind-up "dancing toys" were crafted after the *Off to See the Wizard* TV characters.

Land of Oz Beech Mountain, Banner Elk, N. C.

Land of Oz Beech Mountain, Banner Elk, N. C.

Land of Oz Beech Mountain, Banner Elk, N. C.

115

Right and below: ABC-TV's 1967-1968 *Off to See the Wizard* cartoon designs spawned merchandising on the largest scale to date. Among the licensed tie-ins: three Craft Master paint kits, four Multiple Toymakers "Rubb'r Nicks," a set of Colorforms, and Mattel's talking puppets and Scarecrow pillow. **Facing page:** The Banner Elk "Land of Oz" park enjoyed a 12-season run atop a North Carolina mountain. It included a tour "through" Oz, displays of memorabilia, and the customary concession and souvenir stands; as shown here, the merchandise ran the gamut.

Right: A 1960s Turkish edition of the 1950s "Classics Illustrated Junior" comic book of *The Wizard of Oz.* **Below:** Ceramic banks of the MGM Oz characters from Arnart Imports (circa late 1960s).

Land of Oz Beech Mountain, Banner Elk, N. C.

Follow the
yellow brick road.

And meet
some real characters.

...ou live it.

Land of Oz

Nº 75104

Oz

ADULT

Passport to Home
Gondola or Bus

Oz Museum

SOUVENIR BOOK

Land of Oz

IN BEAUTIFUL
NATURAL COLOR

Above: Ad brochure, souvenir
book, and ticket stub from
Banner Elk's "Land of Oz." A
fire, vandalism, and dwindling
attendance led to the park's
demise after the summer
of 1980, but the site was
reopened for an occasional
private event (and on a much
more informal scale) in the
late 1990s.

EASE on DOWN the ROAD

While the 1970s brought new Oz films, a smashingly successful Broadway musical, and a profusion of products and publications, MGM's *Wizard* continued to dominate the scene. Even a two-season theatrical reissue on a Saturday/Sunday matinee basis couldn't minimize its ongoing television success; by 1980, *Oz* had been shown 22 times — invariably as the top-rated program in its time slot. The 1970 telecast paid brief homage to the film's star when host Gregory Peck eulogized, "Judy Garland left a legacy of performances perhaps unequaled by any star of our time." When MGM auctioned its costumes and props later that year, the bid for Garland's ruby slippers topped all other sales at $15,000.

By now, the MGM treatment of *Oz* had become so ingrained in public consciousness that it was an integral part of daily American life. (Indeed, as early as 1970, it was estimated that more people had seen *Oz* than any other entertainment in history.) Parodies and paraphrases of its dialogue laced countless TV and film scripts, editorials, newscasts, and sermons. An accompanying acceleration in merchandising was thus inevitable and, whether MGM- or Baum-inspired, there were new coloring and comic books, collector's plates, Halloween costumes, figurines, decoupage and toiletry kits — even a prototype bedroom suite of Oz furniture and fabric. The most notable new products arrived in 1975-1976 when Mego debuted their film-inspired Oz dolls and accompanying playsets of the Emerald City, Witch's Castle, and Munchkinland.

Although the later Oz books were quietly allowed to go out-of-print in the 1970s, Baum's 14 titles and many of his other fantasies were reissued again and again. His far-reaching appeal was particularly evidenced by the nonstop promulgation of foreign language editions of the Oz stories; by 1976 there had even been five original Oz

Above: Window card poster for the weekend reissue appearances of MGM's *Oz* in 1970-1971. **Facing page:** Mego dolls patterned after the MGM characters pose before the Witch's Castle, one of three playsets the company created for children in 1975-1976.

books written in Russian by Alexandr Volkov. (Volkov first adapted
The Wizard of Oz into Russian in
1939 and at that time — though
cursorily acknowledging Baum —
took primary credit for the narrative himself.)

Dedicated as ever, the thriv-
ing International Wizard of Oz
Club championed an English
translation of Volkov's first sequel
in 1969 and really hit their
stride by publishing two final
manuscripts by Ruth Plumly
Thompson: *Yankee in Oz* (1972)
and *The Enchanted Island of
Oz* (1976). In 1971, they also
began printing a magazine of
members' fiction, assembled
and issued annually as *Oziana*.

Not surprisingly, there were by this time a number of impre-
sarios who originated Oz entertainments in hopes of matching the
success of MGM's film. (Not surprisingly, most of them failed.)
Cinetron's *The Wonderful Land of Oz* — seen only in brief matinee
appearances in 1969-1970 — was the first of several washouts. Produced and directed by Barry Mahon, the film was adapted from the
second Oz book and damned by disinterest from children coast-to-
coast; it quickly disappeared.

A similar fate befell a more ambitious project several years later.
Producer Norman Prescott had recorded the songs and dialogue for a
feature-length *Return to the Land of Oz* cartoon in 1962, and its poten-
tial seemed better than promising. The score was written by Sammy
Cahn and James Van Heusen, and the cast of star voices included
Ethel Merman, Danny Thomas, Milton Berle, Rise Stevens, Paul Lynde,
and Margaret Hamilton. Prescott's real coup came when he signed
16-year-old Liza Minnelli for the role of Dorothy. Unfortunately, with
only 11 minutes of finished footage, he ran out of money; it took
10 years to complete the animation. The retitled *Journey Back to Oz*
came and went at theaters in the United Kingdom in 1972, in the
United States in 1974, and was soon thereafter relegated to afternoon
television.

Above: The Singer Company
spent two million dollars to
sponsor and promote the
annual *Oz* telecast in 1970.
In addition, they distributed
free *Oz* posters and sold a
repackaged edition of the
soundtrack album.

There was, however, life after MGM, and it took a pop/rock score, an awe-inspiring production, and a vibrant African-American cast to prove it. *The Wiz* came to Broadway in January 1975 with little advance publicity and no advance sale; the producers posted a provisional closing notice on opening night. But elated word-of-mouth and a quickly (but brilliantly) produced TV commercial overcame both the show's somewhat shallow approach to the emotions of the story and the mixed critical notices. In the words of its hit song, *The Wiz* induced audiences to "ease on down the road" for four years and 1,672 exhilarating performances. Unfortunately, the contemporary tone of its humor and a misbegotten 1978 film adaptation dimmed any prospects of longevity for the property. But in its original Broadway incarnation, *The Wiz* was not only glorious fun but further demonstration of the everyman-adaptability and truth of Baum's original narrative.

Below: Singer's ad for the 1970 telecast. The company also donated $25 thousand to the Los Angeles Motion Picture Country House and Hospital and commissioned a Norman Rockwell painting of MGM's Dorothy and Toto, all in honor of Judy Garland, who had died the preceding year.

Above: Promotional cel for *Journey Back to Oz* (1974), the full-length cartoon in which Mombi the Witch conquered the Emerald City with a herd of giant green elephants. The film was in production from 1962-1972; character voices were supplied by Mickey Rooney, Herschel Bernardi, Jack E. Leonard, and Paul Ford. **Left:** A label for *Oz* firecrackers from Macau. **Facing page:** Press-book cover for the 1969-70 matinee feature, *The Wonderful Land of Oz*.

Facing page: The Manhattan Transit Authority promoted the New York subway system with this 1978 poster. Dorothy and the Cowardly Lion from *The Wiz* are shown in company with (among others) Melba Moore, Eartha Kitt, Monte Markham, Betsy Palmer, Martin Balsam, Carol Channing, Reid Shelton, and cast members from *The Magic Show, Grease,* and *Beatlemania*. **Below:** Souvenir program for Broadway's *The Wiz* (1975). **Right and above:** Teaser poster and premiere ticket for the film version of the show (1978). The ad art changed considerably between the advance promotion and actual debut, but nothing could save the $30 million flop.

THE WIZ

THE MOVIE!
Coming This Fall From Universal Pictures

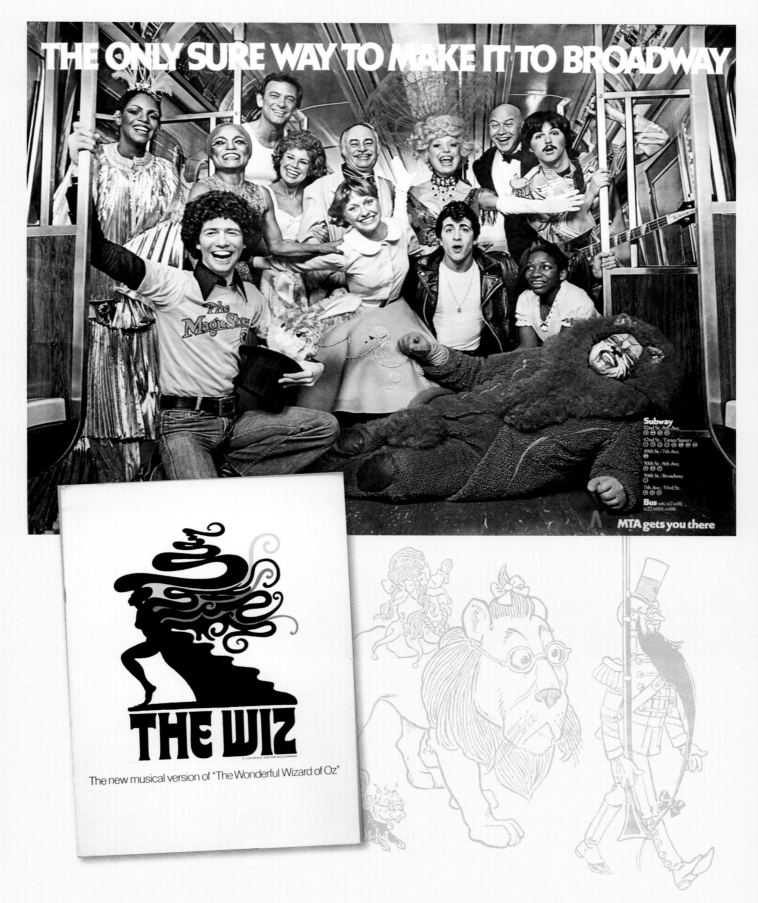

Top: With the increased proliferation of products in the 1970s, it was easy for entire rooms to be done over in Oz décor. Even Christmas trees could be Oz-themed after Kurt S. Adler, Inc., began marketing the first of its series of Ozzy holiday ornaments. **Above:** "Pop art" wood composition statues, MGM-inspired, and posed on contemporary Oz fabric.

RETURN to OZ

All roads led to the Emerald City in the 1980s; an Ozian omnipresence saturated the decade. Baby boomers who had grown to love the story on television or in the public domain book-push 20 years earlier were now sharing it with their own families — or their consumers. Astoundingly to some, happily to all, its cross-generational appeal never faltered, whether proffered as an at-home pleasure, a theatrical adventure, or a shopping opportunity. The personalities of Baum's magic world kept pace with every developing trend in presentation.

There was, by this time, more quantity than quality in much of the output. Home video only added to the prospects for film and television productions, but most of the contemporary efforts had as little prospect for longevity as their immediate predecessors. In the growing category of "more curious than classic": an animated *Thanksgiving in the Land of Oz* (1980), an original 30-minute TV special with Sid Caesar as the voice of the Wizard;

Above: A Spanish sticker book retold *The Wizard of Oz* with scenes from the 1986 Cinar cartoon series. **Below:** Cinar-inspired toy PVC figures from Spain (1988). **Facing page:** International *Return to Oz* memorabilia (all circa 1985), clockwise from top: Australian standee display, Japanese theater program, German comic book, Japanese Heart & Heart toy figurines, and British drinking mugs (a premium from Total Motor Oil).

The Wizard of Oz (1983), a Japanese feature redubbed for American audiences with Lorne Greene as the voice of the Wizard; and *Dorothy Meets Ozma of Oz* (1988), a 30-minute retelling of the third Oz book — without the Wizard. Rankin/Bass did a fine "animagic" adaptation of Baum's *The Life and Adventures of Santa Claus* for CBS-TV (1985), although their somewhat somber treatment precluded its revival as an annual holiday event. In 1988, Jim Henson went as far back as *Mother Goose In Prose* when announcing a string of his own Baum-inspired children's programs.

The most ambitious series of video presentations to date arrived in 1986 when Canada's Cinar Films introduced four feature-length cartoons — *The Wonderful Wizard of Oz*, *The Marvelous Land of Oz*, *Ozma of Oz*, and *The Emerald City of Oz* — assembled from 52 half-hour Oz adventures. (The latter also were offered separately in their entirety as television programming.) Neither narration by Margot Kidder nor the major investment in storytelling time could overcome the dreary animation and Cinar's curious propensity for unnecessarily rewriting Baum's plots and devices.

The real Oz continued to find its outlet in bookstores, especially when Del Rey made available mass-market paperbacks of the 14 Baum titles and (briefly) reprinted 15 of the 19 Thompson books as well. By this time, there were also countless original Oz stories written and (for the most part) privately printed by fans themselves. An outstanding contrast to the amateur efforts appeared in Eric Shanower's fine "graphic novels," written and drawn for First Comics, and in two more

Above: More of the international merchandising inspired by *Return to Oz*: The Dorothy doll was crafted by Zapf Puppen in Germany, while her companions came from Heart & Heart in Japan.

Top: The Greek poster for *Return to Oz.* **Above:** "Keep On Dreamin'" was a new song added as underscoring to the film's end credits in Japan and released there as a single. **Right:** This British picture puzzle imaginatively pictured an all-star Oz cast in a harrowing setting.

For Wieland with all my love — Maurice Sendak   Nov. 29. 82

Oz Club publications: *The Forbidden Fountain of Oz* (1980) by Eloise Jarvis McGraw and Lauren Lynn McGraw, and *The Ozmapolitan of Oz* (1986) by Dick Martin.

In the decade's most important enterprise, the Disney Studios launched themselves into Ozian territory after 30 years of aspiration. (Walt Disney acquired film rights to a dozen Baum Oz titles in 1956, originally intending to star TV's "Mouseketeers" in a 1957 musical, *Rainbow Road to Oz*.) In 1985, Disney produced a much-heralded, $27 million live-action *Return to Oz*; the results were bittersweet. Extremely well-cast, the picture offered visually breathtaking representations of the Baum/Neill concepts of Oz, including first-rate character re-creations, expert "Claymation" incarnations of the gnomes, and the indelible image of the Gump as it flew across the moon. Unfortunately, a dark and almost humorless script sank the film as joyless, emotionally uninvolving entertainment for a mass audience. Though more successful abroad than in the United States, *Return to Oz* was a

Above: Original Maurice Sendak pre-production character concept art for *Return to Oz*, inscribed by the legendary illustrator. This is one of only three pieces he created before departing the production.

mystery in its heavy-handed approach to a lighthearted land.

Part of its demise could be traced to the ongoing ardor felt by so many for the MGM film, which remained a public delight. Even a 1980 home video release didn't preclude another decade of ratings triumph for the Garland picture as an annual television event. The magic diversified as well. In 1987, London's Royal Shakespeare Company premiered a stage presentation that, for the first time, utilized both the film score and screenplay. Its reception led to a less-successful arena tour in the United States (1989), emblazoned by special effects, but sunk by an entirely prerecorded acting/singing soundtrack for the "live" cast. Original movie memorabilia continued to command headline-making prices at auction, culminating in a $165,000 bid for a pair of ruby slippers in 1988. And even MGM was astounded at the outpouring of emotion and media attention generated by the film's 50th anniversary in 1989. At the height of the hoopla, the Library of Congress and National Film Registry announced that *The Wizard of Oz* was one of the first 25 motion pictures to be designated a "National Treasure."

Above: The happily carved portion of Jack Pumpkinhead, here made of Fiberglass and utilized on-screen in *Return to Oz* for the sequence in which Jack's head and body temporarily are separated. **Below:** Baked clay maquettes of the Scarecrow, a Wheeler, Tik-Tok, and Jack Pumpkinhead — the first three-dimensional stage of preparations for their *Return to Oz* characterizations.

Left: French posters tout two of the film's "ExtraOZdinaire" personalities. **Below:** Fairuza Balk's ruby slippers from *Return to Oz*. Used via special (and expensive) licensing from MGM, the Disney shoes were later awarded as the prize in a magazine contest — much as one pair of the 1939 footwear was won by teenage Roberta Bauman in 1940.

Right: Worldwide theatrical productions of *The Wizard of Oz* began to multiply in the 1960s and culminated with the debut of the Royal Shakespeare adaptation of the MGM film in London in 1987. *The Wizard of Oz Live!* (1989) was an ambitious, arena-scaled variation of the movie, but its lackluster prerecorded dialogue, songs, and music disappointed audiences; much of the show's scheduled tour was canceled. **Below:** *The Wizard of Oz* appears onstage in Poland (1991).

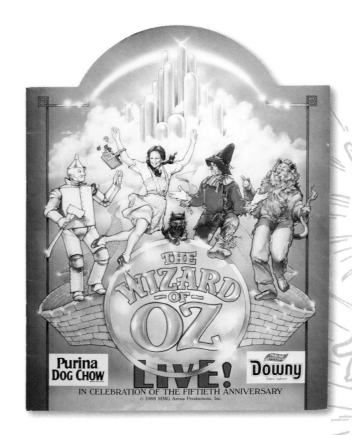

Above: Downy Fabric Softener helped promote the 1989 VHS tape release that celebrated the 50th anniversary of MGM's *Wizard*. But their rebate certificate was so beautifully designed that most people didn't redeem it.

Left: Macy's department store in New York City sponsored three weeks of in-house *Oz* anniversary events and festooned their Herald Square store with Ozzy statues, flags, clocks, and carpeting.

139

Left: These 50th anniversary music boxes were available only in Japan. **Below:** *Return to Oz* collectibles (1985). The top right Tik-Tok figurine was an instant scarcity, created solely as a souvenir for those who attended the film's British premiere. The Royal Army of Oz medallion (center) was another promotional keepsake, as were all three Oz keys — the latter provided as mementos for the movie crew. The remaining items, molded plastic character pins, were sold at Tokyo Disneyland.

Facing page: Oz Music Boxes (clockwise from bottom right): Dorothy and Glinda (1981) and Dorothy in the Haunted Forest (1983) from Seymour Mann; book-inspired characters made in Japan (circa early 1970s); Dorothy and the Scarecrow (circa 1970s); Dorothy and the Tin Woodman from Schmid (1983); Dorothy and Toto from Spencer Gifts (1974); the Tin Woodman from Seymour Mann (1981); the Scarecrow and Lion from Schmid (1983, center rear); the Lion, Dorothy, and Scarecrow from Seymour Mann (1981).

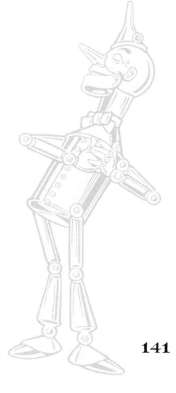

Rainbow Road

When other twentieth century icons hit their special anniversaries, they savored a flurry of excitement and merchandising, followed by the public's swift segue to the next celebration. *The Wizard of Oz* proved a singular exception to tradition. After (or because of) the 1989 tumult, both the MGM film and Baum's world only gained in momentum as esteemed and (sometimes even nicely) exploited properties.

The legend and licensing of MGM's *Oz* never stopped. Already a 1980s best-seller, the film videotape soared to cumulative sales of six million units by 1998. At Orlando's Disney/ MGM Studios Theme Park, the climax of their Great Movie Ride came in its saunter through Oz. The United States Postal Service put Judy Garland and Toto on a 1990 stamp in commemoration of major films of 1939. The same year also brought a Saturday morning network cartoon series, utilizing the movie characterizations and sound-alike voices.

When the Las Vegas MGM Grand Hotel opened in 1993, an Oz motif was everywhere apparent in its décor and attractions. Adaptations of the film continued to appear as "live" events: a benefit *The Wizard of Oz In Concert*, televised from New York's Lincoln Center (1995); a touring and television special *The Wizard of Oz On Ice* (which debuted in 1995); and both full-length and condensed versions of the Royal Shakespeare script, which played virtually everywhere.

There were welcome variations from the MGMania. NBC offered a glowing TV movie, *The Dreamer of Oz*, for Christmas 1990, and

Above: Poster for the Museum of the Moving Image at the British Film Institute in London. By the 1990s, MGM's *The Wizard of Oz* had come to symbolize (as few other films could) the Golden Age of Hollywood; it was one of the very few motion pictures of any era that was happily familiar to all ages. **Facing page:** Mounted together on an Ozzy base, each Silvestri snow globe depicted a different highlight of Dorothy's adventure (1995).

Above: Merchandise from "The Oz Kids" Store, Tokyo's exclusive marketplace for products inspired by the animated TV series (1995). The "Tin Boy" and "Scarecrow, Jr." figures on the right are one-of-a-kind, non-commercial maquettes, created at Hyperion Entertainment as preliminary models for the two cartoon characters. **Right:** Souvenirs and promotional material from the Oz-oriented era of the Las Vegas MGM Grand Hotel (1993-1996).

BG-2085/218-104

despite slightly rewritten history and a few slow sequences, the Baum biographical drama was a stylish, warmly performed endeavor. Earlier that year, the Frances Goldwyn Library in Hollywood mounted a Baum exhibition — one of many assembled on behalf of Oz and/or its creators all over the country by the 1990s. Paul Taylor's *Oz*, an original ballet based on Baum characters, premiered at New York's City Center in 1992. In 1993, the Oz Club added another "official" book to the series by publishing *The Wicked Witch of Oz* by Rachel Cosgrove Payes, designed and illustrated in best tradition by Eric Shanower.

The decade also brought an inspired approach to Oz animation when Hyperion Studio produced 26 episodes of *The Oz Kids* (1995). The innovative concept followed the adventures of the offspring of the

Above: An animation cel and matching background from the Saturday morning TV series based on MGM's *The Wizard of Oz* (1990-1991). As early as 1961, Metro had manifested (unfulfilled) interest in producing its own Oz cartoons, with Judy Garland once again vocalizing for Dorothy Gale. With all of the 1939 principal cast having passed away by the 1990s, the finally-realized animated program instead cast vocal doubles for the major Ozians.

Below: Between 1980 and 1998, the MGM film received multiple repackagings for the home video market, first on tape, then on laser disc, and finally on DVD. (Since then, *Oz* has enjoyed at least three further, major restorations and remasterings, resulting in its availability on Blu-ray and in 3D.) **Facing page:** The United States Postal Service celebrated four classic 1939 movies with these blocks of first-class stamps (1990). Sixteen years later, Judy Garland was honored in the USPS "Legends of Hollywood" series, and the actual stamp art pictured her at the time of *A Star is Born* (1954). But the selvage on which the stamps were mounted offered a glowing portrait of her Dorothy of Oz.

famous Baum characters; so popular were the programs in Japan that an "Oz Kids" Store was established there. Individual shows were later combined into eight feature-length videos for sale in the United States and abroad.

Garnering additional attention in the 1990s were the well-established "Oz Festivals" that first sprang up during the preceding decade. Anywhere from 10,000 to 60,000 people annually attended weekend events in Chittenango, New York (Baum's birthplace); Grand Rapids, Minnesota (Garland's birthplace); and — especially — Chesterton, Indiana, where a gift shop and museum had evolved into a virtual "Oz Central" for Midwesterners. The major attraction at each gathering was the appearance, "in person," of surviving Munchkin actors from the MGM film.

In Liberal, Kansas, a vintage farm dwelling was reconfigured as "Dorothy's House," drawing year-round tourists. Baum himself was actively heralded as a native son in special celebrations in Aberdeen, South Dakota, despite the author's comparatively brief residency (1888—1891) as a shopkeeper and newspaper editor. But historians correctly noted that the description of a drought-and-tornado-plagued Kansas in the opening chapter of the first Oz book was drawn from Baum's actual experience during his years in the Dakotas.

Finally, to the accompaniment of affectionate audience and media farewells, the network television contracts for MGM's *Oz* finally lapsed in 1998 after the film's 39th telecast in 42 years. (The property was assured a future home on cable.) To herald its approaching 60th anniversary, *The Wizard of Oz* was booked into 1,800 theaters in autumn 1998, quickly adding $14 million to its box office gross.

Left: Promotional poster for the TV movie/biopic, *The Dreamer of Oz,* in which John Ritter forsook his usual comedic turns to effectively and compassionately portray L. Frank Baum. **Below:** First issues of *Oz Squad* and *Oz,* alternative "dark side" graphic novels (1995). **Facing page:** Creature Features and sculptor Tony McVey of Menagerie Productions skillfully collaborated on this collectible resin model kit of an horrific winged monkey (1996).

Left: Souvenir program for the 90-minute stage version of the MGM film that played New York's Madison Square Garden in 1997. The initial engagement featured TV's Roseanne as Miss Gulch/The Wicked Witch of the West; in succeeding seasons, she was followed by everyone from Jo Anne Worley to Eartha Kitt. (The role of Professor Marvel/The Wizard was often taken by Mickey Rooney.) **Below left:** This 1992 German production had an original script but used the MGM score. **Below:** The 1994 Israeli *Wizard* had new songs except for "Over the Rainbow." There was even a Dorothy/Barbie modeled on Michal Yannai, the popular Israeli singer who starred in the show. **Facing page:** *The Wizard of Oz On Ice* featured a prerecorded soundtrack on which all character voices except Dorothy were performed by comic Bobby McFerrin (1995).

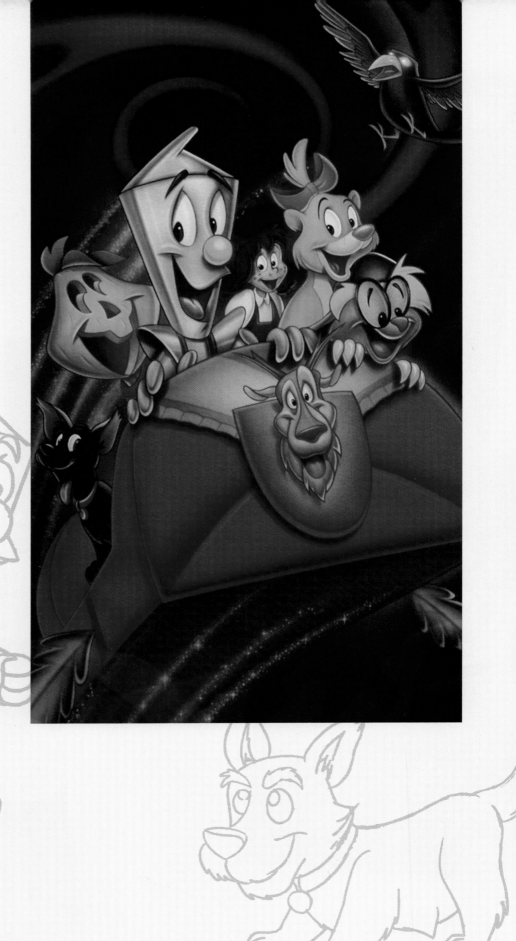

Right: Cover art for The Oz Kids video, *The Return of Mombi* (1996). Among those who gave voice to "the Kids" in various episodes of the series were future TV stars Jonathan Taylor Thomas of *Home Improvement* and Benjamin Salisbury of *The Nanny*.

Facing page: The first century of Oz came full circle when the 1990s Oz Kids character pins perched atop the open pages of a 1900 first edition of *The Wonderful Wizard of Oz*.

SO MUCH HAPPENED BEFORE DOROTHY DROPPED IN.

KRISTIN CHENOWETH   IDINA MENZEL

AND

JOEL GREY
AS THE WIZARD

A NEW MUSICAL

WICKED

THE UNTOLD STORY OF THE WITCHES OF OZ

KRISTIN CHENOWETH   IDINA MENZEL in WICKED
Music and Lyrics by STEPHEN SCHWARTZ   Book by
WINNIE HOLZMAN   Based on the novel by GREGORY MAGUIRE
Also Starring CAROLE SHELLEY   NORBERT LEO BUTZ and JOEL GREY
Musical Staging by WAYNE CILENTO   Directed by JOE MANTELLO

CALL TICKETMASTER: (212) 307-4100 • ⇒N⇐ GERSHWIN THEATRE, 222 WEST 51st ST.

WICKED WONDERFUL

As if its first magical century were mere overture, Oz enjoyed a fresh combination of presentation, product, and public fascination in its second millennium. This was vividly underscored when two new creative works provoked an especially triumphant international response.

Even those signal successes were but peaks of the perpetual fervor for all things Oz. There was a new, seemingly ceaseless spate of Oz-related books. Widely diverse, the journalese included adept or inept Baum biographies; a definitive expansion of *The Annotated Wizard of Oz*; MGM Munchkin autobiographies; murkily-detailed political, financial, or psychological analyses; a floodtide of professional or self-published (and sometimes adroit) fan fiction; bibliographies; cookbooks; colorful facsimiles of original editions; Oz texts minus all or most of their illustrations; and graphic novels. The violent, aggressively dark tenor of many of the latter was offset by Skottie Young's faithful depiction of the earliest Oz stories in a comic book format scripted by Eric Shanower. By 2013, the two award-winning artists had covered six Baum titles, the first volumes of which achieved rank on *The New York Times* Best Seller list. Oz book reprints increasingly appeared as well in both lavish and modest foreign editions, with Russia's Sergei Sukhinov continuing the original tales published years earlier by Alexandr Volkov.

Meanwhile, Baum's creation continued to permeate all popular media, if in sundry fashion. The SyFy Channel's *Tin Man* (2007) attracted that network's largest miniseries audience, though receiving mixed reviews for a gloomy, adult treatment of fantasy. Not unexpectedly, *The Muppets' Wizard of Oz* (2005) was more family-friendly and Baum-y, if at times irreverent. Oz segments, parodies, and allusions saturated commercials (touting everything from Federal Express to M&Ms); hundreds of editorial cartoons and comic strips; scores of

Above: The best-selling collaboration of Skottie Young and Eric Shanower retold Baum's story in graphic novel form (2009). Their approach won the men two 2010 Eisner Awards for "Best Limited Series or Story Arc" and "Best Publication for Kids." **Facing page:** Since its premiere in 2003, *Wicked* has become an international stage sensation. Kristin Chenoweth and Idina Menzel toplined the original cast, inspiring fan mania and setting the standard for those singing actresses who've succeeded them as Glinda and Elphaba.

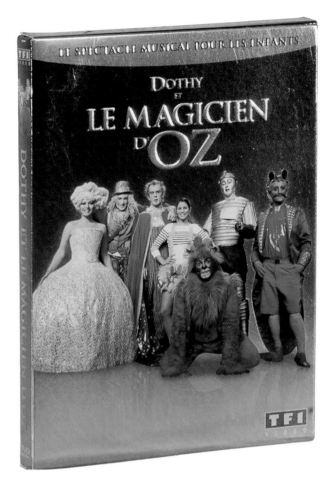

Above: The DVD of the original French musical arena show, *Dorothy and the Wizard of Oz* (2009). **Facing page:** The SyFy cable TV channel mini-series, *Tin Man*, was publicized in this graphic novel by Moore and Thomas (2007). The $20 million, four-and-a-half hour dark approach to Oz won both adherents and detractors; its stars included Zooey Deschanel as "DG," Alan Cumming as "Glitch," Richard Dreyfus as "the Mystic Man," and Wyatt Cain in the title role.

motion pictures; and such satirical television programs as *The Daily Show* and *Saturday Night Live*. More seriously, the 2005 *Yellow Brick Road* documentary highlighted the affecting real-life tale of a troupe of disabled actors as they prepared an Oz production, and the Smithsonian Channel endeavored to explain *The Origins of Oz* (2010). Most ambitious among hundreds of stage shows was Sir Andrew Lloyd-Webber's reworking of the MGM script and score, for which he conducted a 2011 BBC-TV talent search for a girl to play Dorothy — and to which he and Tim Rice added new songs. After a lengthy London Palladium engagement, their adaptation began a North American circuit in 2013.

Homage on a more historical level came with a series of Oz exhibitions, effectively squelching any residue of the library/educator apathy of earlier decades. From Kansas City, Missouri, to Wausaukee, Wisconsin, private collectors set up temporary or permanent showcases of their holdings. In Amherst, Massachusetts, the Eric Carle Museum of Picture Book Art displayed "The Wonderful Art of Oz" (2006): 72 original pieces by 19 artists, ranging from Denslow and Neill to Andy Warhol and Maurice Sendak. Six years earlier, the Los Angeles Central Library drew record-setting crowds when it celebrated "A Century of Oz: Selections from The Willard Carroll Collection" (which serves as the basis for this book). In "The Wizard of Oz: An American Fairy Tale" (2000), the Library of Congress most tellingly paid similar tribute, acknowledging "the literary achievements of one of the most creative authors of the twentieth century." Eleven years later, the Library again celebrated Baum's first Oz title as one of "the books that shaped America."

On a smaller scale, Oz also and easily lent itself to specially-produced interactive children's exhibitions, several of which toured the country. The first full-time Oz museum opened — not surprisingly — in Kansas in 2004, where the village of Wamego joined the list of other locales that offered an annual weekend Oz festival. By 2013, some of those events were in their fourth decade, continuing to draw crowds in the tens of thousands and exhilarating children who

A Century of OZ

Selections from The Willard Carroll Collection

Above and right: "A Century of Oz" attracted record-setting crowds as "Selections from the Willard Carroll Collection" celebrated the centennial — and far-reaching effects and ephemera — of Baum's creation. The exhibition invitation included its own souvenir bookmark; both boasted Denslow artwork (2000).

A Century of OZ

Selections from The Willard Carroll Collection

November 4, 2000 to February 24, 2001

CENTRAL LIBRARY
Getty Gallery

LOS ANGELES
PUBLIC LIBRARY

were the offspring of original attendees. Surviving MGM Munchkins remained a major attraction on such occasions until age gradually prevented their attendance.

Throughout, the initial introduction to Baum's world remained the 1939 motion picture, which somehow gained luster with (and maintained its emotional hold on) each new generation. After acquiring the film in its merger with Turner Broadcasting, Warner Bros. launched the film into multiple annual cablecasts and home video re-issues. They repeatedly employed state-of-the-art picture and sound restorations for *Oz*, presenting it in a rapturously-received Blu-ray DVD in 2009. Anticipating its 75th anniversary, the picture was reconfigured in 3D for 2013-14 release. Warner Bros. also dove into a much-expanded and stringently-monitored merchandising program. By 2013, the result was a pretty much incalculable flood of quality-controlled goods, delighting both rabid collectors and gentle aficionados. Non-MGM Oz images remained in the public domain, which created an almost equal outpouring of alternate products.

Recognition and respect for the film and its components never flagged. *The Wizard of Oz* came in at #10 on the American Film Institute's 2007 survey of the greatest American motion pictures. In other polls, it placed as AFI's number one "best fantasy" and number three "best musical"; in 2004, voters rated Judy Garland's rendition of "Over the Rainbow" as the number one film song of all time. "Rainbow" won an equal honor when categorized as the number one "Song of the [Twentieth] Century" in a 2001 poll conducted by the National Endowment for the Arts and the Recording Industry Association of America. Even the rival Sony Pictures Entertainment — ensconced in the former MGM Studios in Culver City, California — got into the act in 2012 by erecting a 94-foot tall, $1.6 million steel rainbow arching over the front gate. A smaller but emotionally more powerful accolade was seen in FilmAid International's video of street children in Kabul, Afghanistan, as they watched a special screening of *Oz* in 2002. Eyes wondrous and shining, the children sat transfixed by their first exposure to film and music, both banned by the Taliban.

Collecting frenzy on the grandest scale continued to rack up fantastic dollar figures for auctioned Oz memorabilia. Typifying the increased fervor for Baum and book items, a signed first edition of *The Wonderful Wizard of Oz* (1900) brought $152,500 in 2002, and an original John R. Neill drawing for *The Scarecrow of Oz* (1915) $16,250 in 2012. The highest prices, however, were accorded the MGM-associated costumes and props. A rubber winged monkey "flying

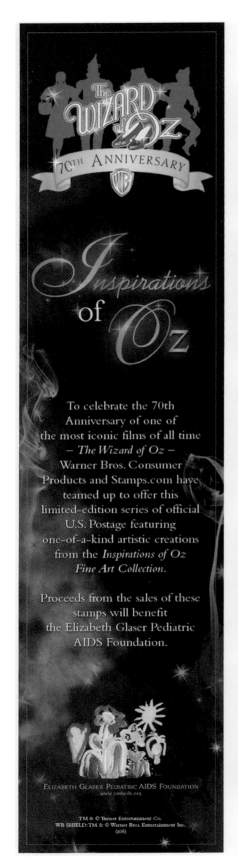

The Wizard of Oz
70TH ANNIVERSARY

Inspirations of Oz

To celebrate the 70th Anniversary of one of the most iconic films of all time – *The Wizard of Oz* – Warner Bros. Consumer Products and Stamps.com have teamed up to offer this limited-edition series of official U.S. Postage featuring one-of-a-kind artistic creations from the *Inspirations of Oz Fine Art Collection*.

Proceeds from the sales of these stamps will benefit the Elizabeth Glaser Pediatric AIDS Foundation.

ELIZABETH GLASER PEDIATRIC AIDS FOUNDATION
www.pedaids.org

TM & © Turner Entertainment Co.
WB SHIELD: TM & © Warner Bros. Entertainment Inc.
(s08)

United States Patents 5,510,992; 5,682,318; 5,717,597; 5,801,944; 5,812,991; 5,819,2

160

miniature" sold for $14,950 in 2005. A Wicked Witch of the West hat leapt in price from $54,625 in 2005 to $206,130 in 2010. Bert Lahr's lion costume went for $700,000 in 2006. A Dorothy pinafore brought $480,000 (2012), while a Dorothy test dress that never appeared in the film sold for $1.1 million (2011). And in 2012 a film industry consortium purchased the best surviving pair of ruby slippers for $2 million for The Academy Museum of Motion Pictures.

Oz thus remained an obvious profit-making powerhouse more than a dozen decades after L. Frank Baum began the saga. Surprising perhaps even its greatest partisans, it also soared higher than ever before in its successful influence on the imaginations of creative professionals. Though somber and revisionist in his approach, Gregory Maguire transmogrified Baum's magic land in a complex, disturbing, and fascinating four-book series. The first title alone, *Wicked* (1996), sold more than five million copies and was followed by *Son of a Witch* (2005), *A Lion Among Men* (2008), and *Out of Oz* (2011). As with the best of earlier Oz "reworkings," Maguire's work captured a cross-generational public. Its attainment was almost immeasurably heightened when portions of *Wicked* were considerably leavened and reconfigured as a Broadway musical.

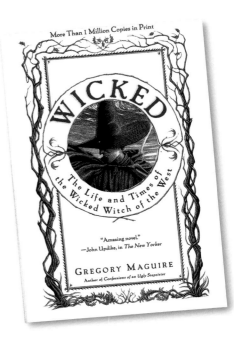

Above: Gregory Maguire's *Wicked* (1995), the book that created its own Ozzy universe while becoming an ongoing sensation for both the publishing industry and world-wide musical theater box office. **Left:** A plush toy winged monkey was one of the first souvenir tie-ins to the stage show, offered for sale in the lobby and on the production's initial web site. **Facing page:** Diverse original art highlighted the commemorative stamp sheet issued by the United States Postal Service as it honored the 70th anniversary of MGM's *The Wizard of Oz* (2009).

Right: The advance poster for Disney's *Oz the Great and Powerful* centered on a glamorous-but-green wicked witch, pointedly appealing to the MGM-familiar expectations of a 2013 audience.

Below: In much-expanded art that accompanied the film's debut, the Ozzy citizenry and landscapes offered a more all-encompassing and evocative come-on. (It worked — to the tune of hundreds of millions of dollars.)

Opening in October 2003, the lavish entertainment won variegated critical reaction but off-the-radar audience raves. Librettist Winnie Holzman and songwriter Stephen Schwartz cleverly walked an emotional tightrope between public familiarity with the MGM film, Baum's concept of country and characters, Maguire's readers, and musical theater aficionados. *Wicked* won three dozen major awards including three Tonys and the Grammy. It remained a box office champion even as it approached its tenth anniversary, surpassing $700 million in Broadway sales and more than $2 billion in its world-wide tours by early 2013. When the New York company added an additional performance during Christmas Week 2012, the show hit an all-time Broadway high: a weekly gross of nearly $3 million for nine shows. *Variety* flatly defined *Wicked* as "a cultural phenomenon."

Magically — Ozzily — enough, there was more to come. With similar faith in Baum's creation (or at least in their own adaptation thereof), The Walt Disney Studios invested $215 million in the 3D motion picture, *Oz the Great and Powerful* (2013). Sam Raimi's mostly original tale of pre-Dorothy history starred James Franco, Mila Kunis,

Above: The "Hello, Kitty" Play-set of Oz dolls as sold in Japan (2008; packaging was similar in the United States). **Below:** Assorted souvenirs from The Land of Oz attraction at Universal Studios Japan amusement park (2006).

Rachel Weisz, and Michelle Williams, and reviewers once again vacillated in response. However, for the first time since 1939, an Oz film became a box office success, ultimately generating a half-billion dollars in world-wide ticket sales. Not surprisingly, the studio quickly announced plans for a sequel.

It now seems safe to state that Oz, its people, its colorful communities and terrain, and its timeless philosophies will never fade from public consciousness — or their happy and conspicuous consumption. In turn, ceaseless credit redounds to L. Frank Baum, his capacity to monumentally regale, and the thrill, uplift, and motivation he provides for other minds. Thanks to his work and stimulus, today's travelers on the Yellow Brick Road continue to acquire limitless, unique passports to excitement, exploration, and matchless remembrance.

The Wonderful World of Oz is thus more than book or story, more than film or stage play, and more than collectibles or emotional intangibles.

Instead, it's become "a real, truly, live place."

And — indeed — an international cultural phenomenon.

Below: A multi-purpose lacquer box from Russia, illustrated with characters from the semi-original Russian Oz books by Alexandr Volkov (circa 2007). **Right:** Depicting a "gorgeously designed collage" of notable Oz art, *The Wizard of Oz* (2009) was a boxed 500-piece jigsaw puzzle tied into *All Things Oz*, a 2003 book that celebrated illustrative material drawn from the Carroll/Wilhite collection.

Facing page: Original magazine illustration by Peter de Sève (circa 2008). The prolific de Sève here follows in the tradition of countless past and present artists by using Baum's characters for political or social commentary — in this case referencing the economic meltdown of the times, as a hapless accountant ("the man behind the curtain") tries to justify and/or repair the damage...and balance the books.

Above: The happy center-spread illustration from the 1949 MGM record of songs from *The Wizard of Oz.*

Acknowledgments: Woolsey Ackerman, Kathleen Fleury, Patty Fricke, Todd Gajdusek, Jon Jankowsky, Kellen Lindblad, Tod Robert Machin, David Maxine, Brent Phillips, Ryan Jay, Lena Tabori, Elaine Willingham. . . . And fellow travelers no longer with us: Dorothy and Jim Nitch, Frederick E. Otto, Rob Roy MacVeigh, Christopher O'Brien, and Fred M. Meyer.

Selected Bibliography

Gardner, Martin, and Russel B. Nye: *The Wizard of Oz and Who He Was* (East Lansing: Michigan State University Press, 1994).

Greene, David L. and Dick Martin: *The Oz Scrapbook* (New York: Random House, 1977).

Hearn, Michael Patrick: *The Annotated Wizard of Oz* (New York: W. W. Norton & Co., 2000; and New York: Clarkson N. Potter, 1973).

Hearn, Michael Patrick, editor: *The Wizard of Oz: The Critical Heritage Edition* (New York: Schocken, 1986).

MacFall, Russell, and Frank Joslyn Baum: *To Please A Child* (Chicago: Reilly & Lee Co., 1961)

St. Johns, Adela Rogers: *Love, Laughter, and Tears: My Hollywood Story* (New York: Doubleday, 1978).

Stone, Fred: *Rolling Stone* (New York: Whittlesey House, 1945).

Swartz, Marc: *Oz Before the Rainbow* (Baltimore: The Johns Hopkins University Press, 2000)

The International Wizard of Oz Club, Inc.: *The Baum Bugle* (1957 to the present). The Club's "Journal of Oz" has tallied over 160 issues in the last 56 years and provides both extraordinary historical research and current information.